ATALANTA

THE RACE AGAINST DESTINY

A GREEK MYTH

GRAPHIC UNIVERSE™

STORY BY
JUSTINE & RON FONTES
PENCILS AND INKS BY
THOMAS YEATES

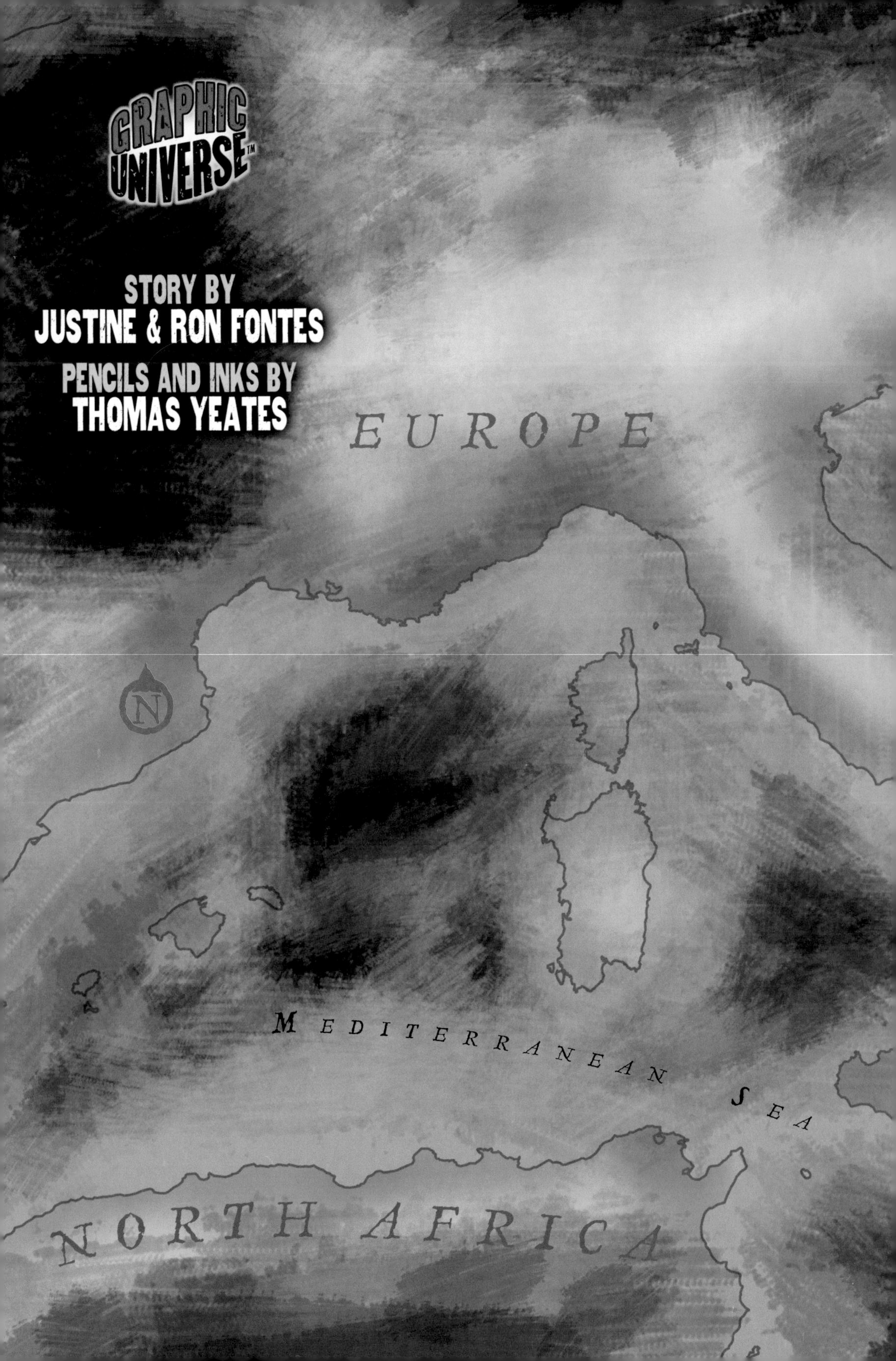

EUROPE
N
MEDITERRANEAN SEA
NORTH AFRICA

ATALANTA

THE RACE AGAINST DESTINY

A GREEK MYTH

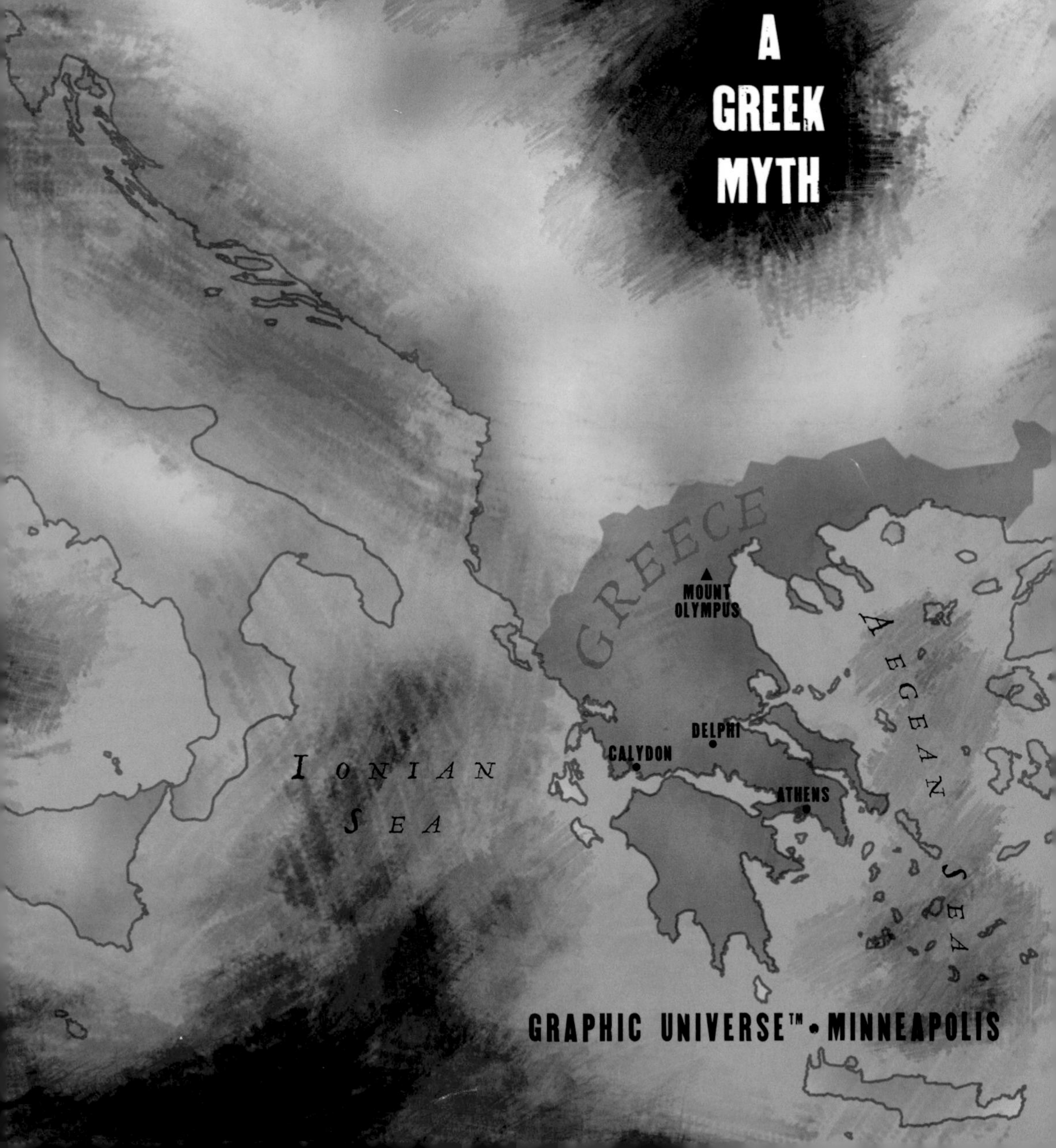
GREECE
MOUNT OLYMPUS
DELPHI
CALYDON
ATHENS
IONIAN SEA
AEGEAN SEA

GRAPHIC UNIVERSE™ • MINNEAPOLIS

THE ancient Greek myths that tell of Atalanta and other heroic figures date back more than two thousand years. The imagery usually associated with Greek mythology is that of Greece's classical period (from about 500 to 323 b.c.), complete with grand temples, flowing garments, and magnificent statues. Atalanta: The Race against Destiny follows that tradition.

Authors Justine and Ron Fontes relied upon many sources, including Edith Hamilton's Mythology and Michael Grant's Myths of the Greeks and Romans. Artist Thomas Yeates used historical and traditional sources for visual details—from images on ancient Greek vases to sculpture and other artwork. David Mulroy of the University of Wisconsin-Milwaukee ensured historical and visual accuracy.

STORY BY JUSTINE AND RON FONTES

PENCILS AND INKS BY THOMAS YEATES,
WITH SPECIAL THANKS TO TOD SMITH,
KEN HOOPER, AND CHRIS MARRINAN

COLORING BY HI-FI DESIGN

LETTERING BY BILL HAUSER

CONSULTANT: DAVID MULROY,
UNIVERSITY OF WISCONSIN-MILWAUKEE

Copyright © 2007 by Lerner Publications Company

Graphic Universe™ is a trademark of Lerner Publications Company.

Graphic Universe™
An imprint of Lerner Publishing Group
241 First Avenue North
Minneapolis, MN 55401 U.S.A.

Website address: www.lernerbooks.com

Library of Congress Cataloging-in-Publication Data

Fontes, Justine.
    Atalanta : the race against destiny : a Greek myth /
story by Justine & Ron Fontes ; pencils and inks by
Thomas Yeates ; coloring by Hi-Fi Design ; lettering
by Bill Hauser.
    p.   cm. — (Graphic myths and legends)
Includes bibliographical references and index.
    ISBN-13: 978-0-8225-5965-8 (lib. bdg. : alk. paper)
    ISBN-10: 0-8225-5965-X (lib. bdg. : alk. paper)
    1. Atalanta (Greek mythology)—Juvenile literature.
I. Fontes, Ron. II. Yeates, Thomas. III. Title.
IV. Series.
BL820.A835F66 2007
398.20938'02—dc22   2006004661

Manufactured in the United States of America
1 2 3 4 5 6 - JR - 12 11 10 09 08 07

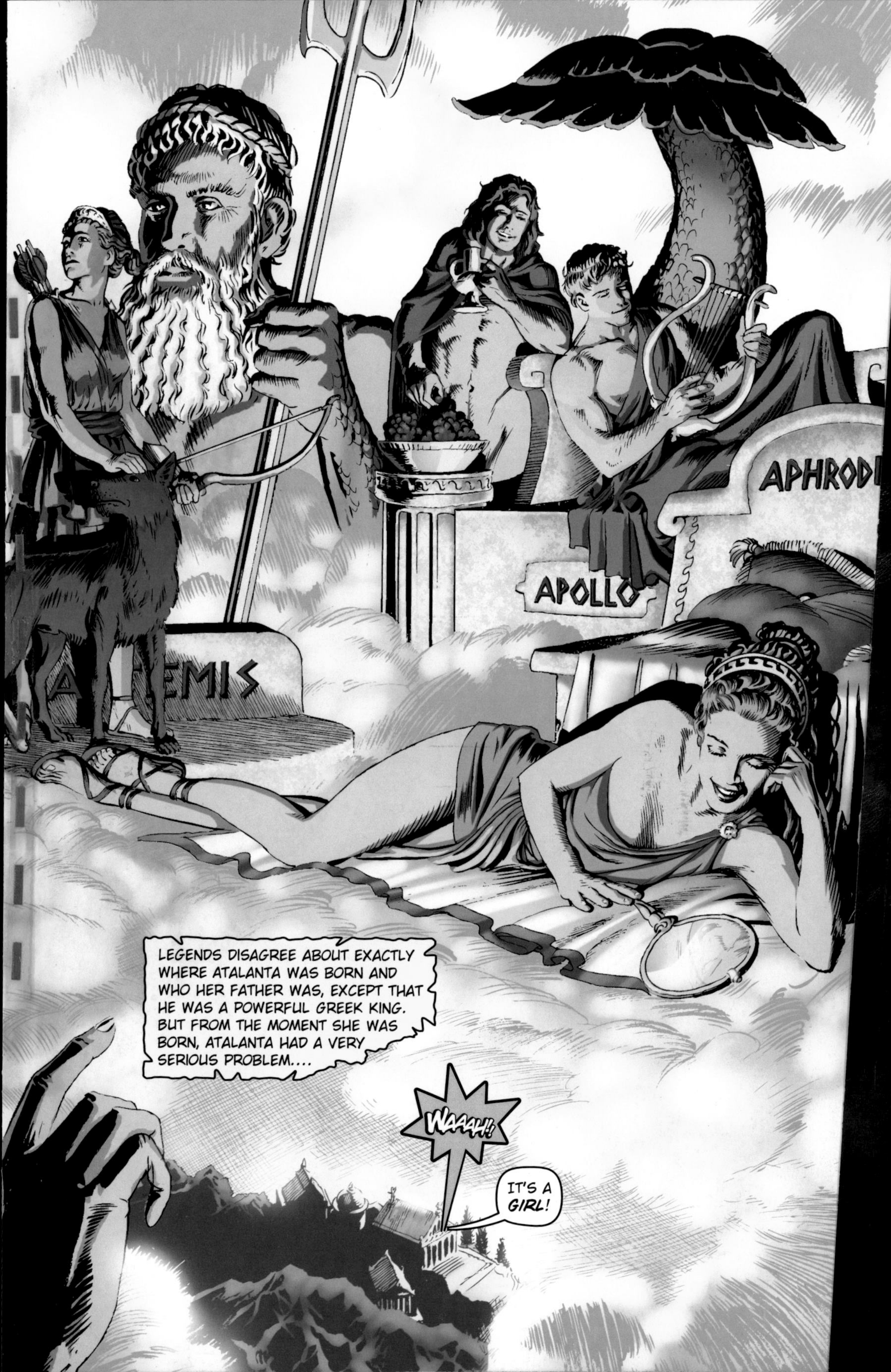
APHRODI
APOLLO
LEGENDS DISAGREE ABOUT EXACTLY WHERE ATALANTA WAS BORN AND WHO HER FATHER WAS, EXCEPT THAT HE WAS A POWERFUL GREEK KING. BUT FROM THE MOMENT SHE WAS BORN, ATALANTA HAD A VERY SERIOUS PROBLEM....
WAAAH!
IT'S A GIRL!

TABLE OF CONTENTS

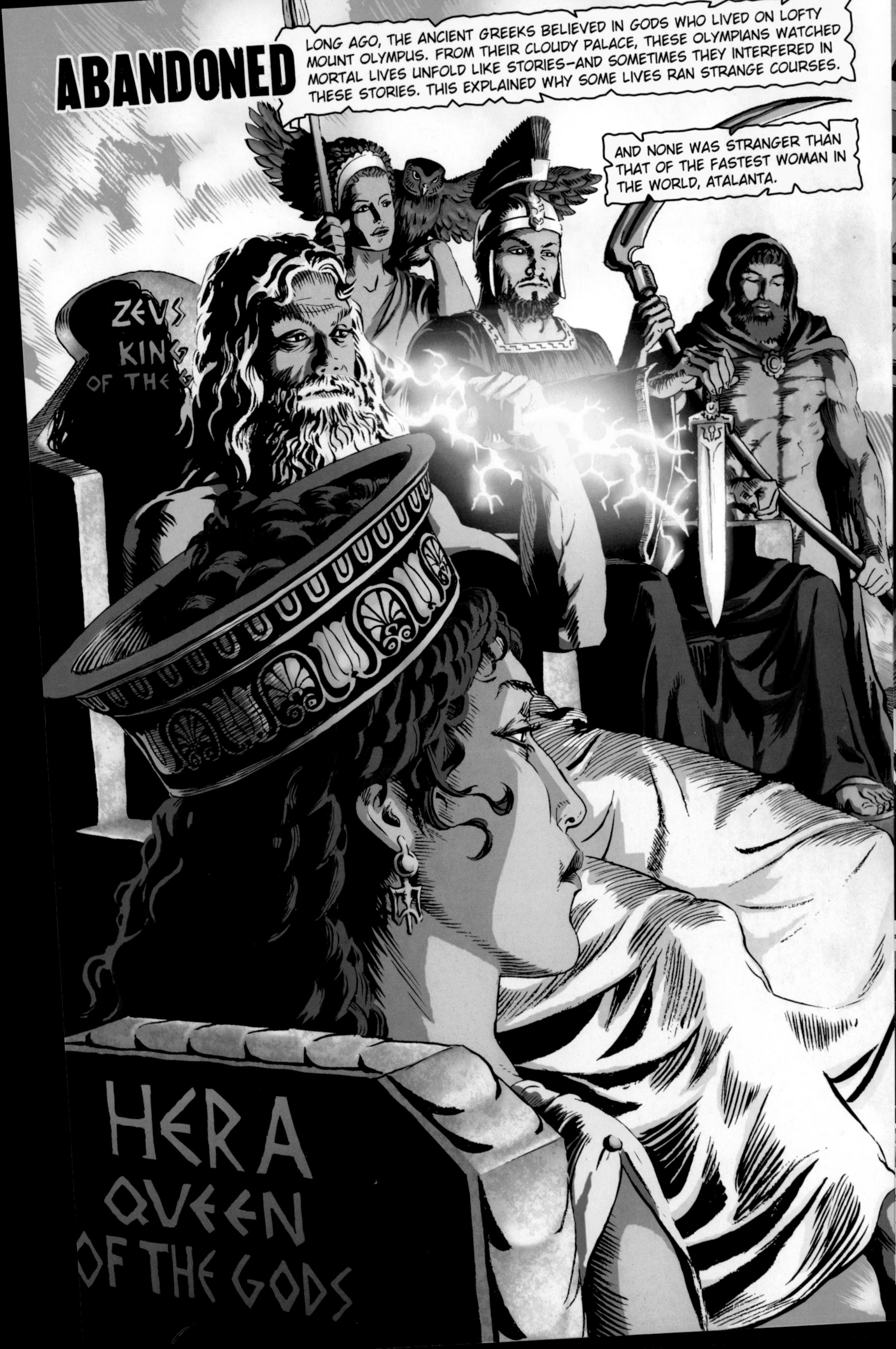
ABANDONED
LONG AGO, THE ANCIENT GREEKS BELIEVED IN GODS WHO LIVED ON LOFTY MOUNT OLYMPUS. FROM THEIR CLOUDY PALACE, THESE OLYMPIANS WATCHED MORTAL LIVES UNFOLD LIKE STORIES—AND SOMETIMES THEY INTERFERED IN THESE STORIES. THIS EXPLAINED WHY SOME LIVES RAN STRANGE COURSES.
AND NONE WAS STRANGER THAN THAT OF THE FASTEST WOMAN IN THE WORLD, ATALANTA.
ZEUS KING OF THE
HERA QUEEN OF THE GODS

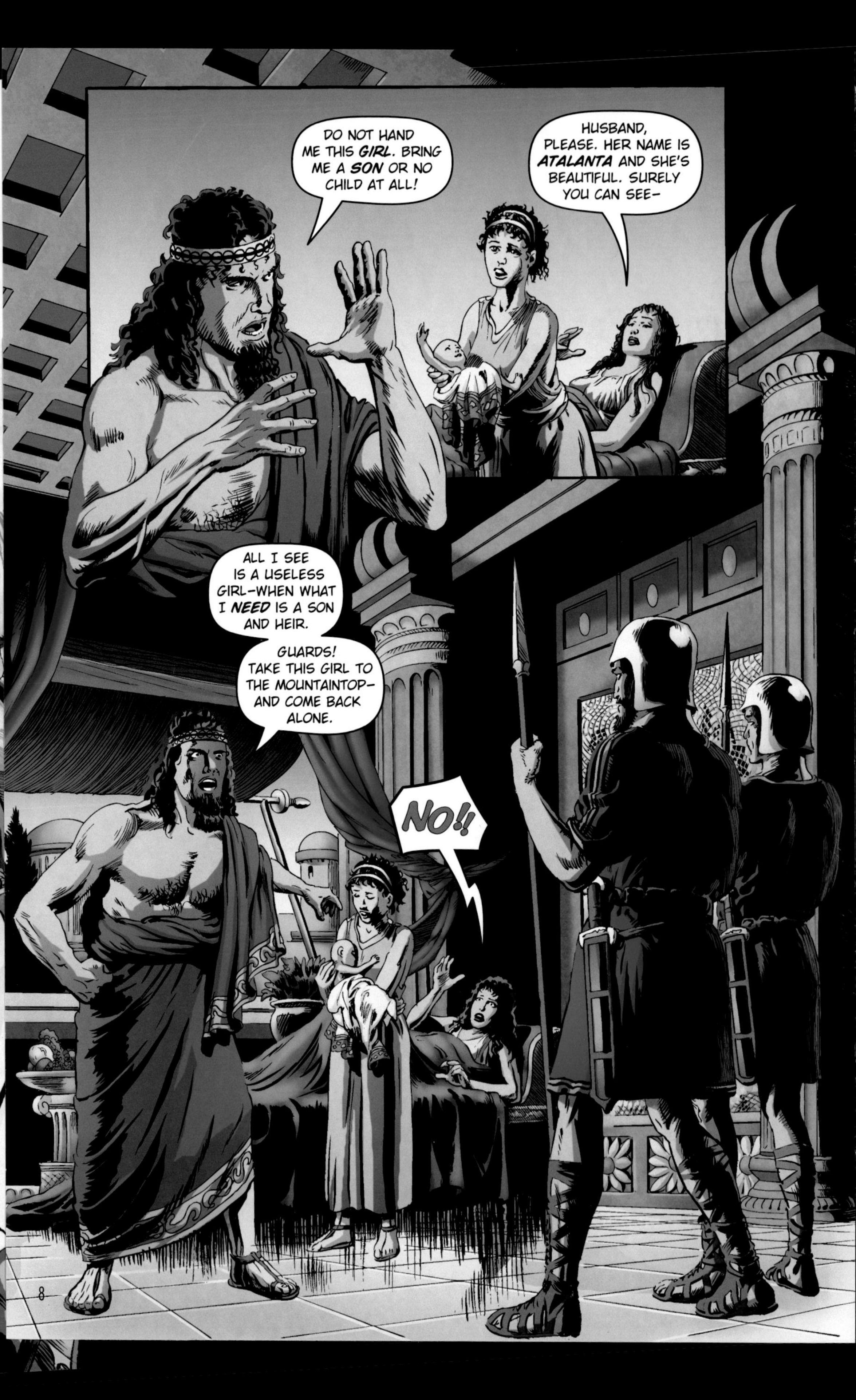
DO NOT HAND ME THIS GIRL. BRING ME A SON OR NO CHILD AT ALL!
HUSBAND, PLEASE. HER NAME IS ATALANTA AND SHE'S BEAUTIFUL. SURELY YOU CAN SEE—
ALL I SEE IS A USELESS GIRL—WHEN WHAT I NEED IS A SON AND HEIR.
GUARDS! TAKE THIS GIRL TO THE MOUNTAINTOP—AND COME BACK ALONE.
NO!!

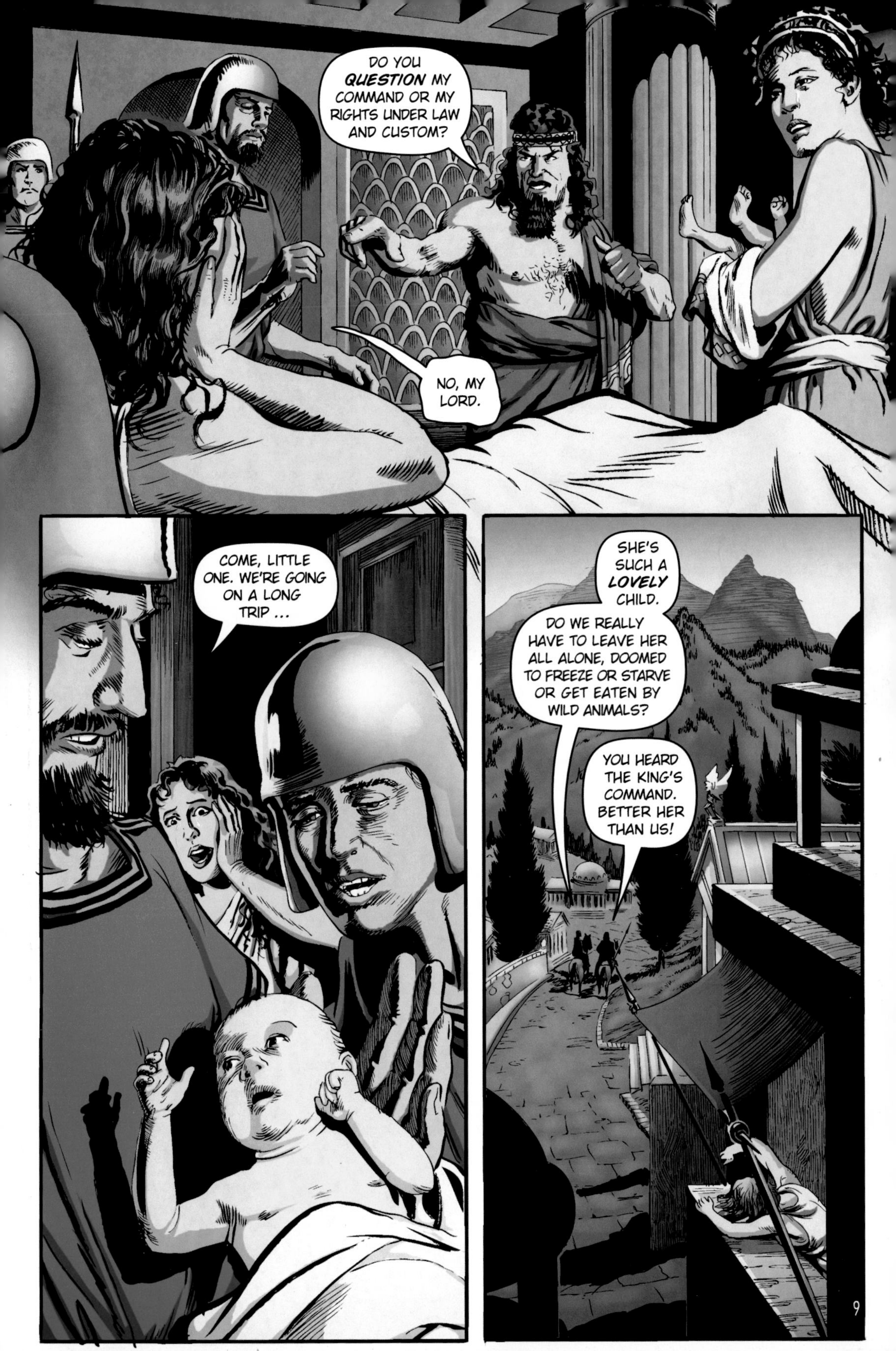
DO YOU QUESTION MY COMMAND OR MY RIGHTS UNDER LAW AND CUSTOM?
NO, MY LORD.
COME, LITTLE ONE. WE'RE GOING ON A LONG TRIP ...
SHE'S SUCH A LOVELY CHILD.
DO WE REALLY HAVE TO LEAVE HER ALL ALONE, DOOMED TO FREEZE OR STARVE OR GET EATEN BY WILD ANIMALS?
YOU HEARD THE KING'S COMMAND. BETTER HER THAN US!

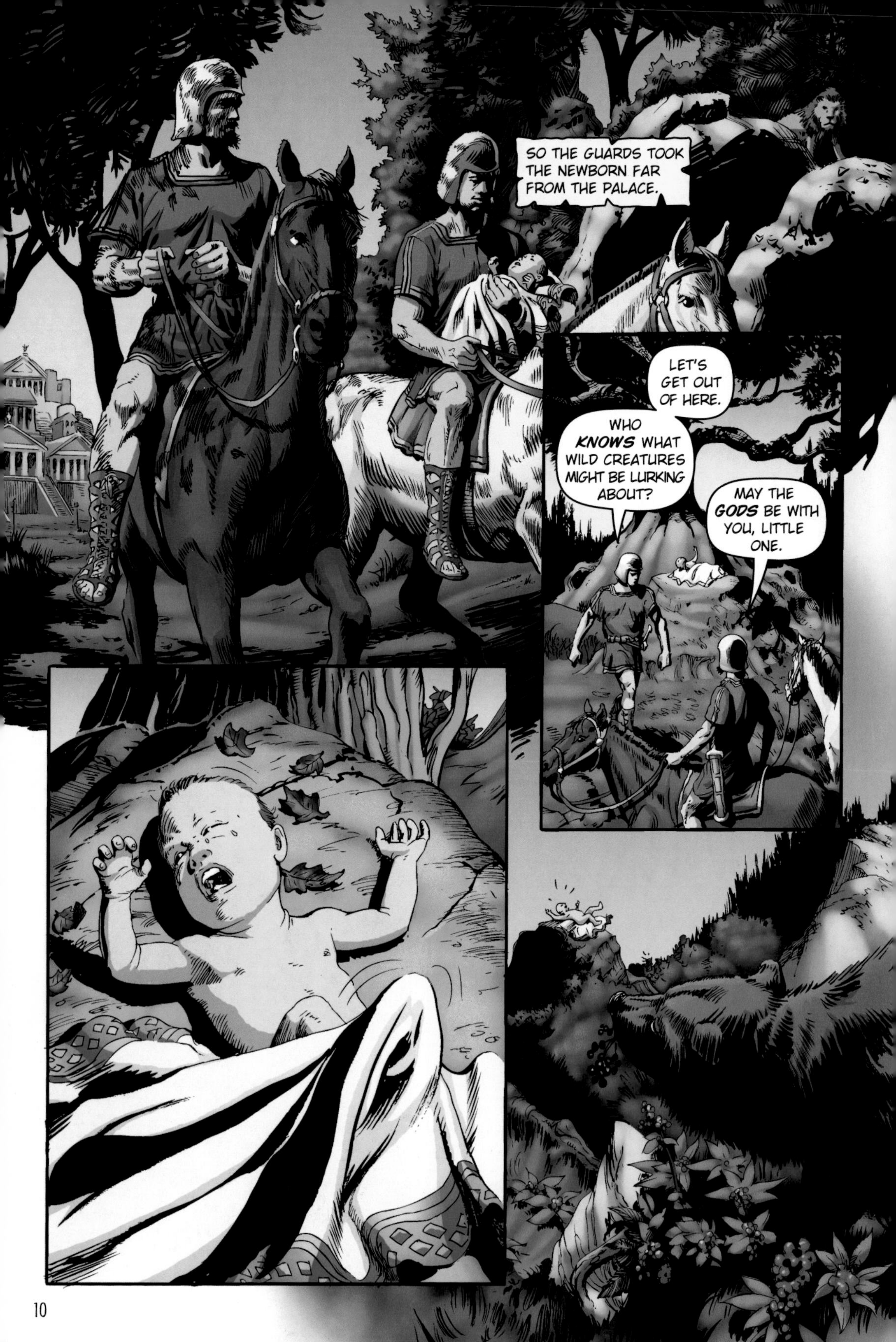
SO THE GUARDS TOOK THE NEWBORN FAR FROM THE PALACE.
LET'S GET OUT OF HERE.
WHO **KNOWS** WHAT WILD CREATURES MIGHT BE LURKING ABOUT?
MAY THE **GODS** BE WITH YOU, LITTLE ONE.

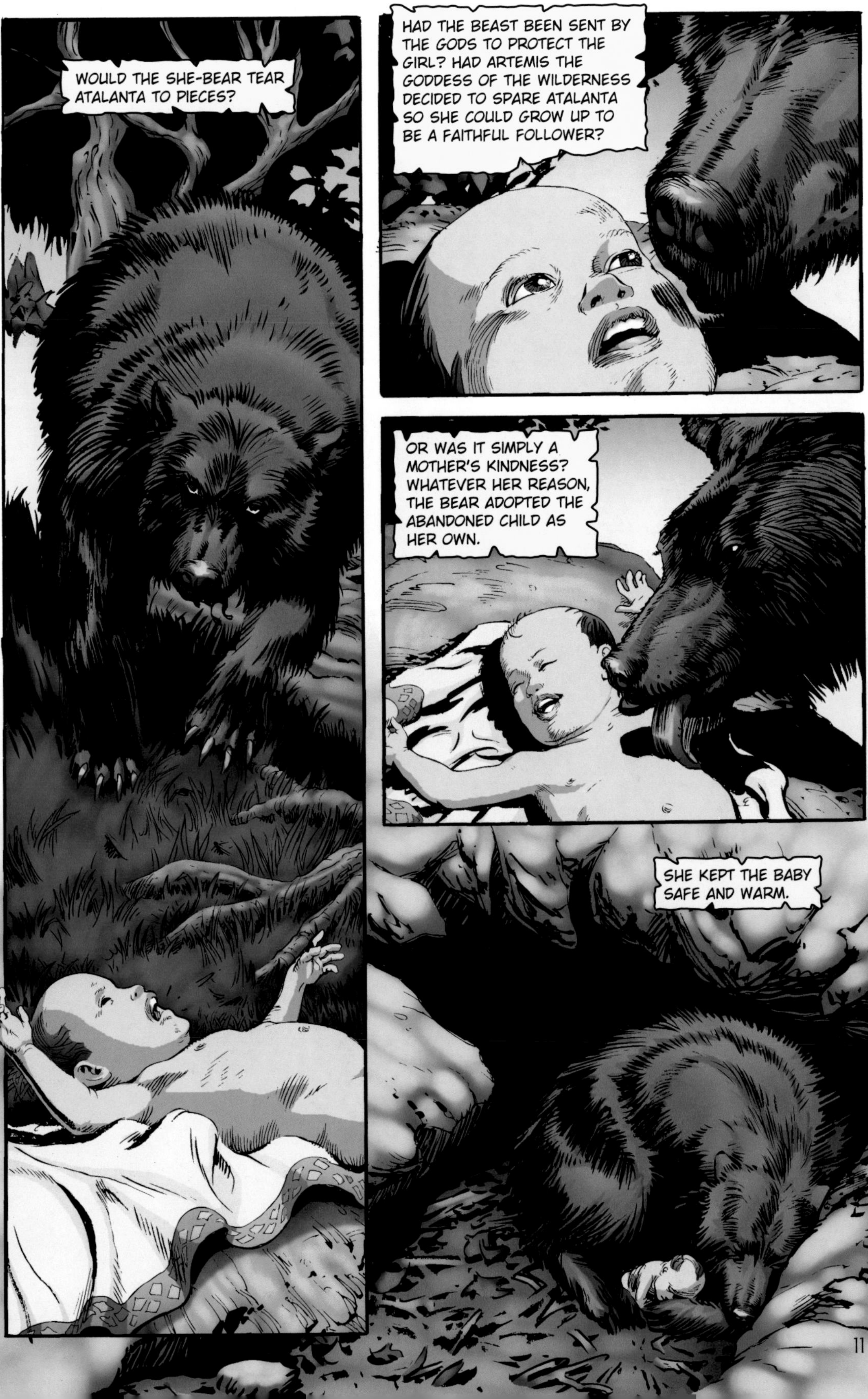
WOULD THE SHE-BEAR TEAR ATALANTA TO PIECES?
HAD THE BEAST BEEN SENT BY THE GODS TO PROTECT THE GIRL? HAD ARTEMIS THE GODDESS OF THE WILDERNESS DECIDED TO SPARE ATALANTA SO SHE COULD GROW UP TO BE A FAITHFUL FOLLOWER?
OR WAS IT SIMPLY A MOTHER'S KINDNESS? WHATEVER HER REASON, THE BEAR ADOPTED THE ABANDONED CHILD AS HER OWN.
SHE KEPT THE BABY SAFE AND WARM.

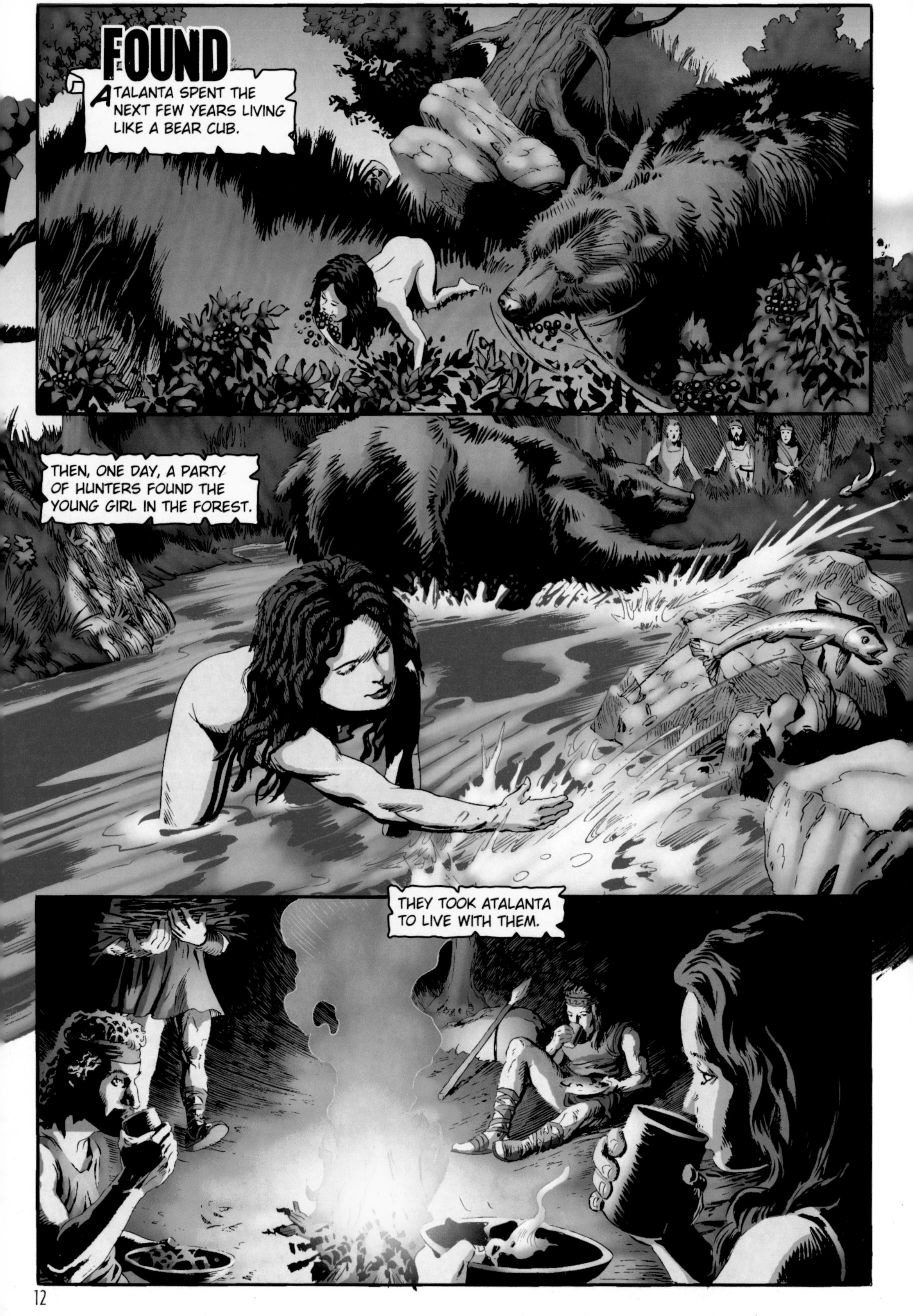
FOUND
ATALANTA SPENT THE NEXT FEW YEARS LIVING LIKE A BEAR CUB.
THEN, ONE DAY, A PARTY OF HUNTERS FOUND THE YOUNG GIRL IN THE FOREST.
THEY TOOK ATALANTA TO LIVE WITH THEM.

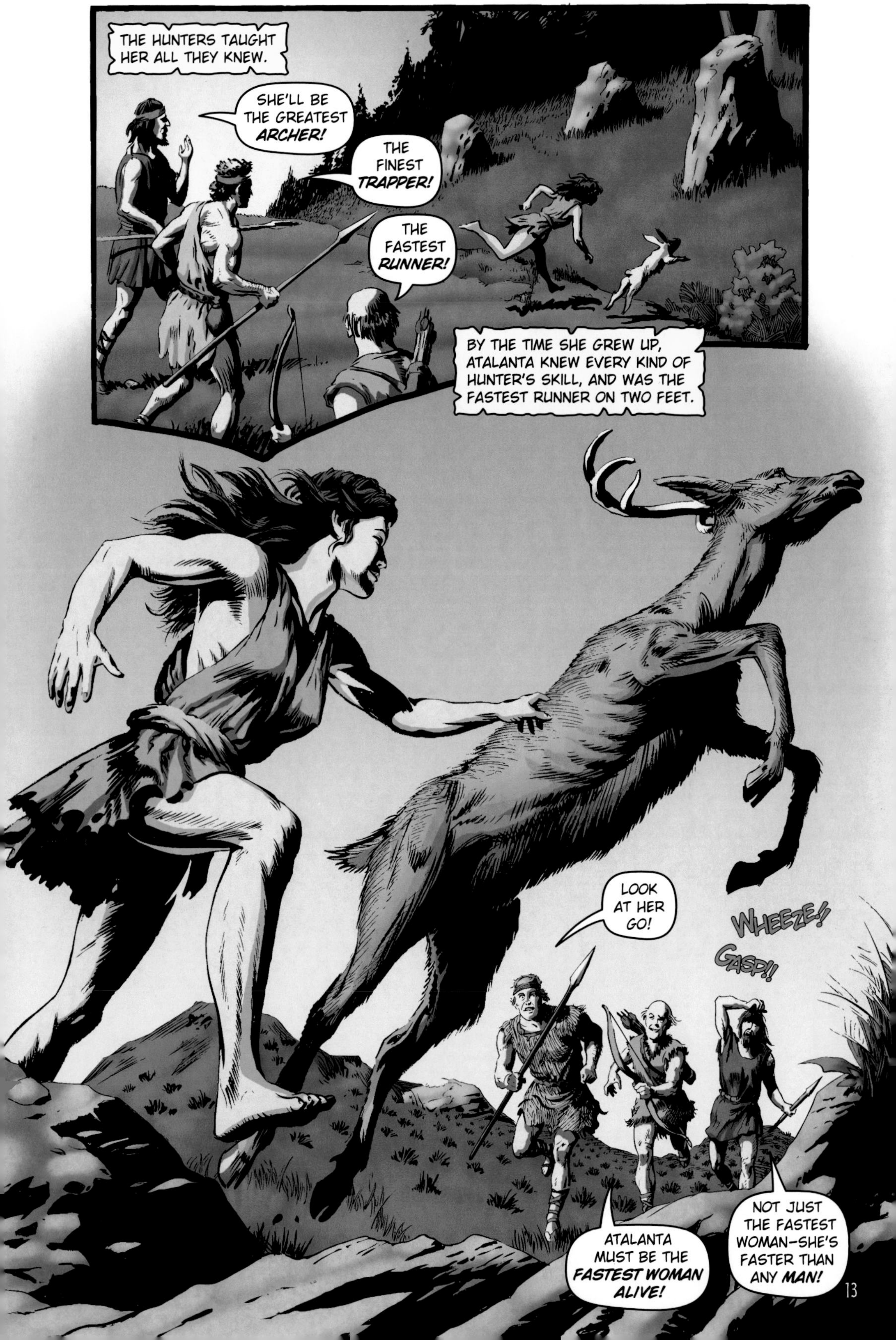
THE HUNTERS TAUGHT HER ALL THEY KNEW.
SHE'LL BE THE GREATEST ARCHER!
THE FINEST TRAPPER!
THE FASTEST RUNNER!
BY THE TIME SHE GREW UP, ATALANTA KNEW EVERY KIND OF HUNTER'S SKILL, AND WAS THE FASTEST RUNNER ON TWO FEET.
LOOK AT HER GO!
WHEEZE!!
GASP!!
ATALANTA MUST BE THE FASTEST WOMAN ALIVE!
NOT JUST THE FASTEST WOMAN—SHE'S FASTER THAN ANY MAN!

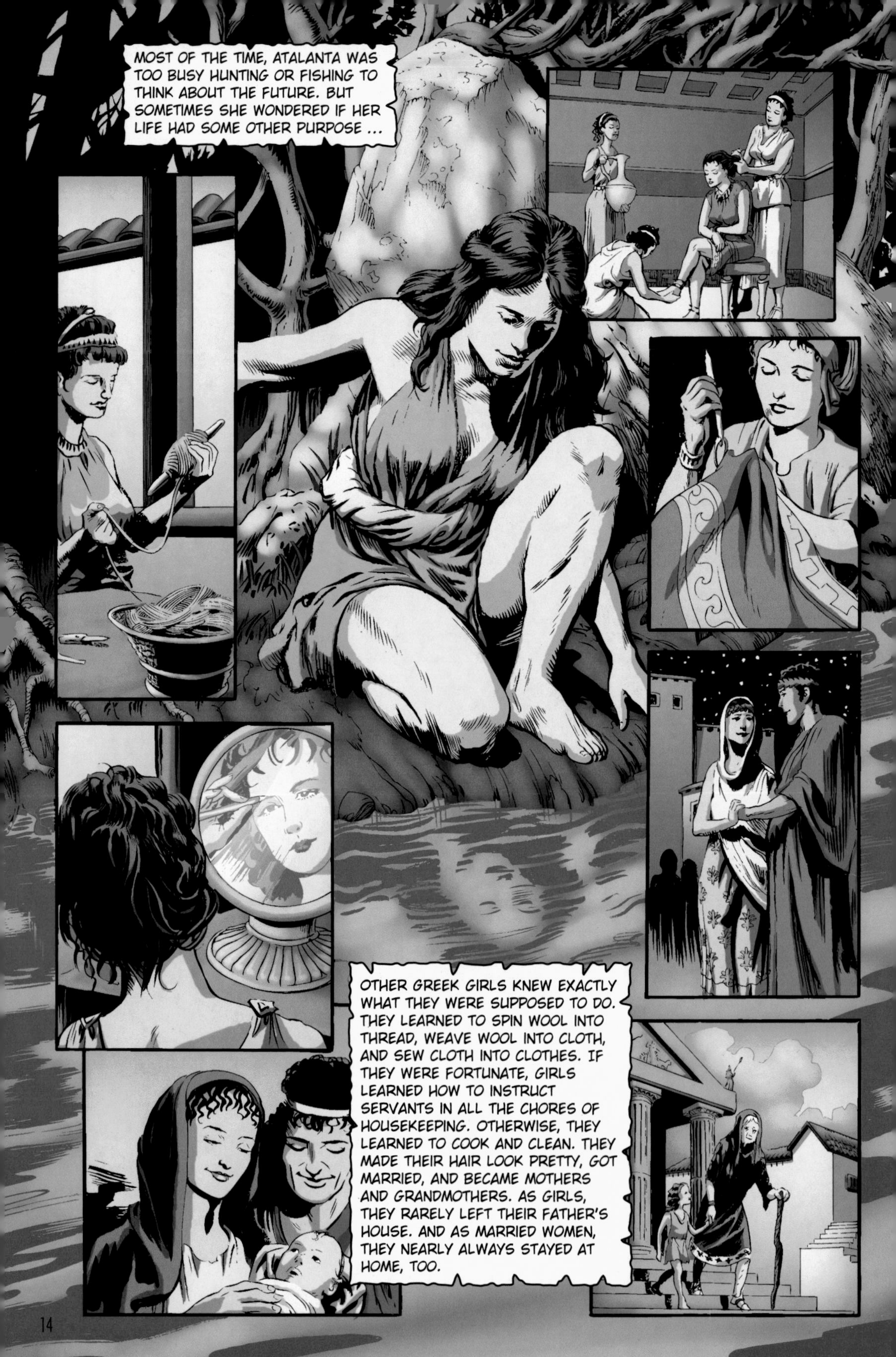
MOST OF THE TIME, ATALANTA WAS TOO BUSY HUNTING OR FISHING TO THINK ABOUT THE FUTURE. BUT SOMETIMES SHE WONDERED IF HER LIFE HAD SOME OTHER PURPOSE ...
OTHER GREEK GIRLS KNEW EXACTLY WHAT THEY WERE SUPPOSED TO DO. THEY LEARNED TO SPIN WOOL INTO THREAD, WEAVE WOOL INTO CLOTH, AND SEW CLOTH INTO CLOTHES. IF THEY WERE FORTUNATE, GIRLS LEARNED HOW TO INSTRUCT SERVANTS IN ALL THE CHORES OF HOUSEKEEPING. OTHERWISE, THEY LEARNED TO COOK AND CLEAN. THEY MADE THEIR HAIR LOOK PRETTY, GOT MARRIED, AND BECAME MOTHERS AND GRANDMOTHERS. AS GIRLS, THEY RARELY LEFT THEIR FATHER'S HOUSE. AND AS MARRIED WOMEN, THEY NEARLY ALWAYS STAYED AT HOME, TOO.

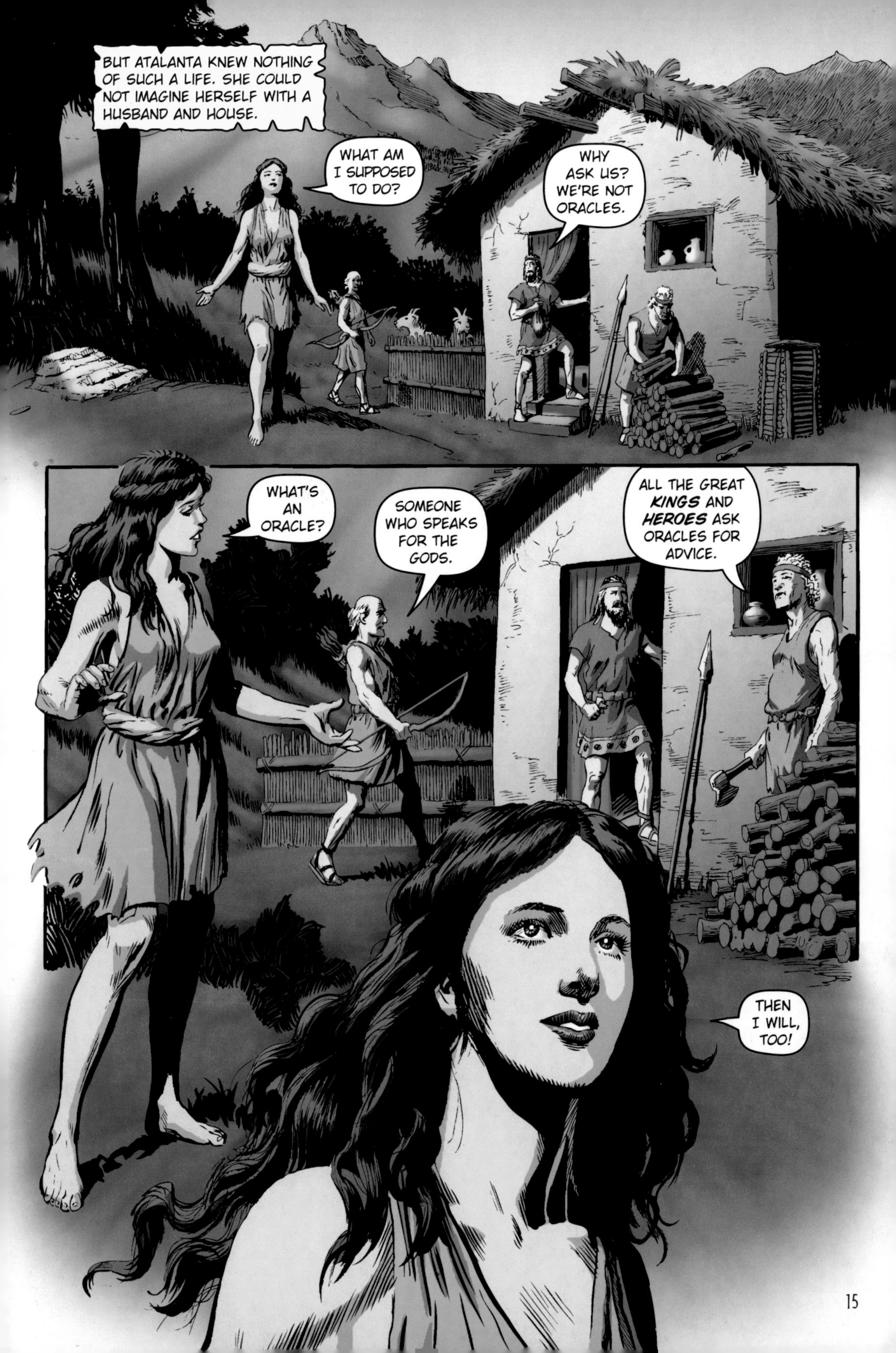
BUT ATALANTA KNEW NOTHING OF SUCH A LIFE. SHE COULD NOT IMAGINE HERSELF WITH A HUSBAND AND HOUSE.
WHAT AM I SUPPOSED TO DO?
WHY ASK US? WE'RE NOT ORACLES.
WHAT'S AN ORACLE?
SOMEONE WHO SPEAKS FOR THE GODS.
ALL THE GREAT KINGS AND HEROES ASK ORACLES FOR ADVICE.
THEN I WILL, TOO!

ANSWERS AND ADVENTURES

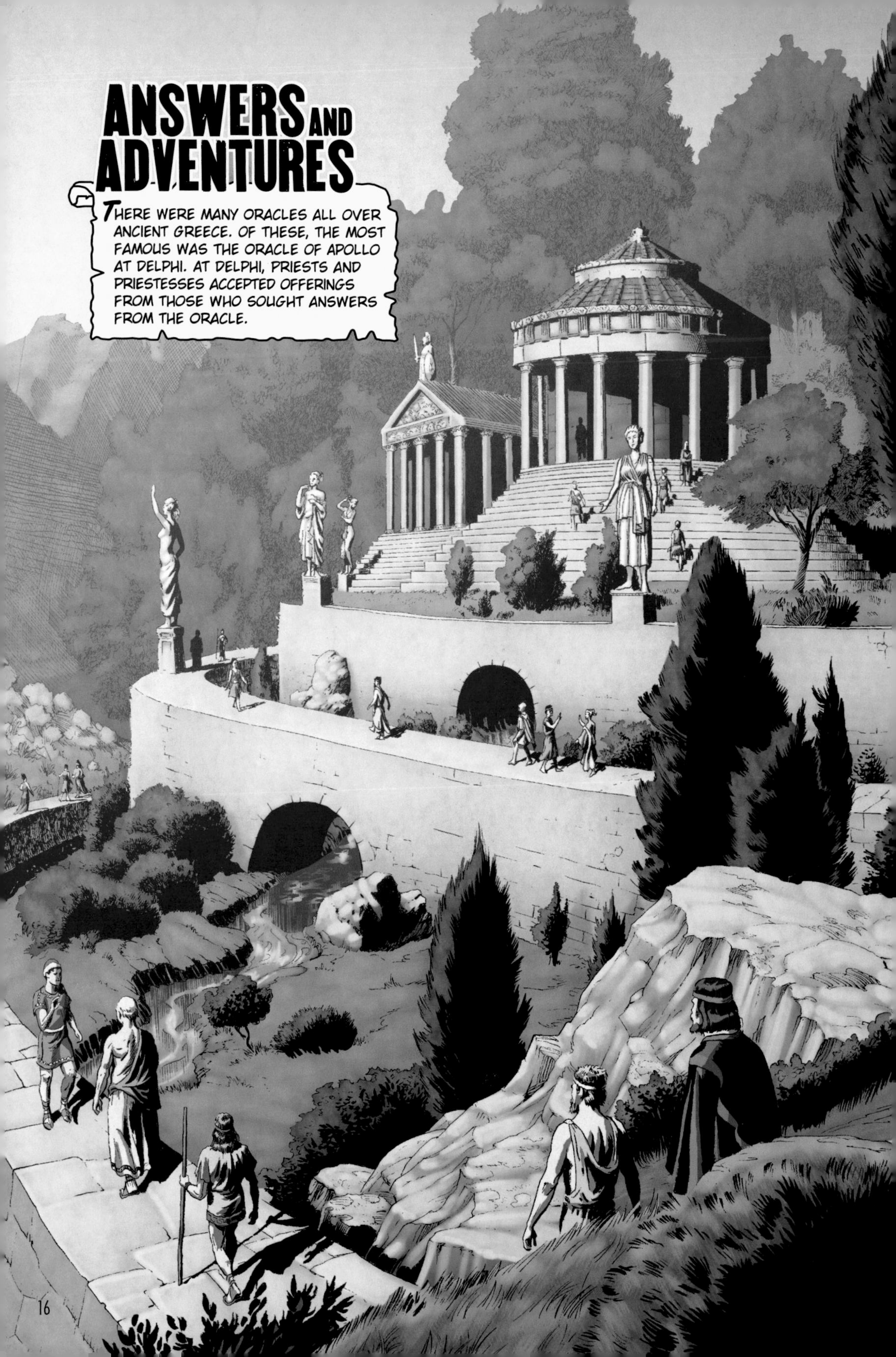
THERE WERE MANY ORACLES ALL OVER ANCIENT GREECE. OF THESE, THE MOST FAMOUS WAS THE ORACLE OF APOLLO AT DELPHI. AT DELPHI, PRIESTS AND PRIESTESSES ACCEPTED OFFERINGS FROM THOSE WHO SOUGHT ANSWERS FROM THE ORACLE.

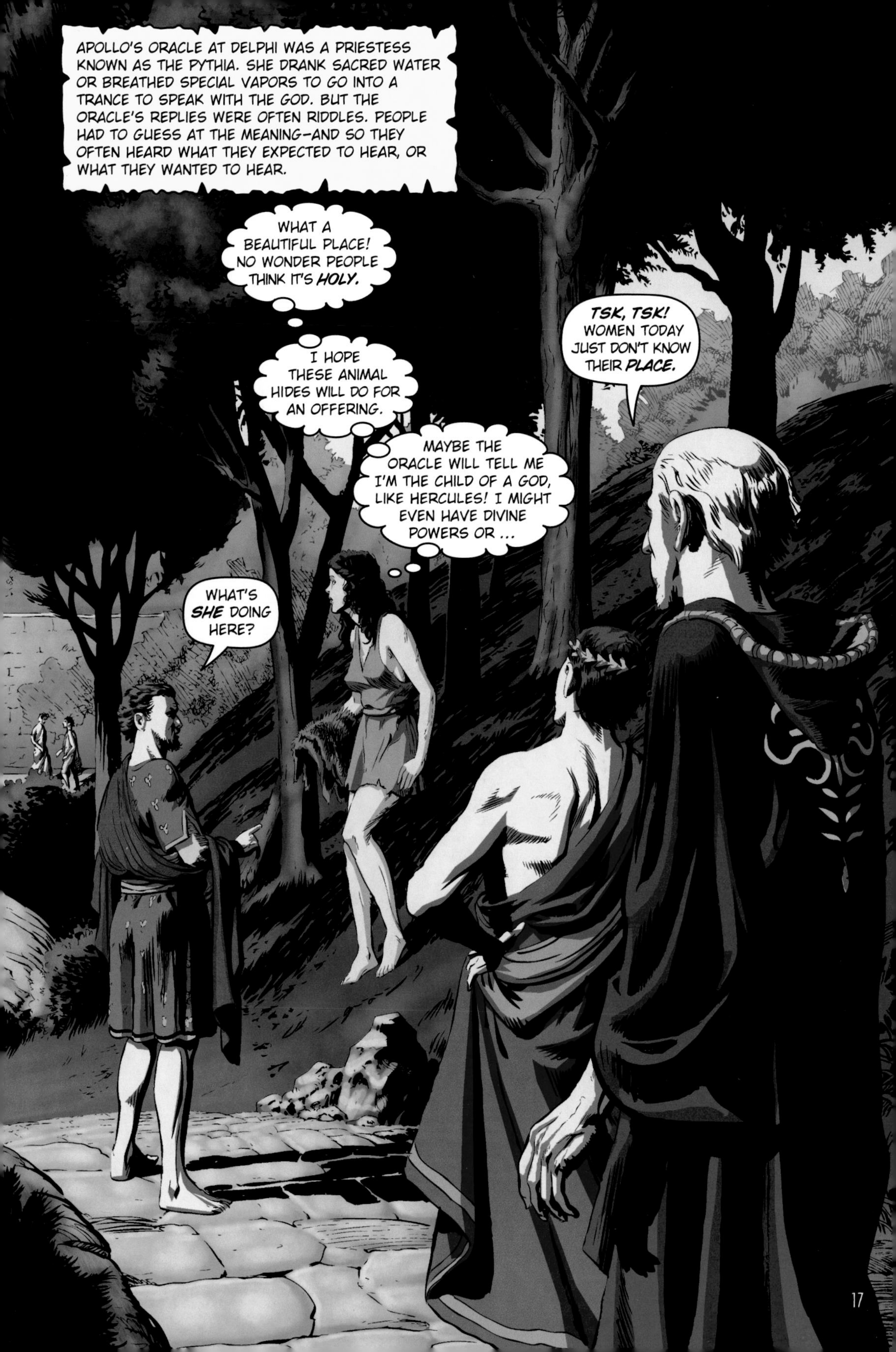

APOLLO'S ORACLE AT DELPHI WAS A PRIESTESS KNOWN AS THE PYTHIA. SHE DRANK SACRED WATER OR BREATHED SPECIAL VAPORS TO GO INTO A TRANCE TO SPEAK WITH THE GOD. BUT THE ORACLE'S REPLIES WERE OFTEN RIDDLES. PEOPLE HAD TO GUESS AT THE MEANING—AND SO THEY OFTEN HEARD WHAT THEY EXPECTED TO HEAR, OR WHAT THEY WANTED TO HEAR.
WHAT A BEAUTIFUL PLACE! NO WONDER PEOPLE THINK IT'S *HOLY.*
I HOPE THESE ANIMAL HIDES WILL DO FOR AN OFFERING.
MAYBE THE ORACLE WILL TELL ME I'M THE CHILD OF A GOD, LIKE HERCULES! I MIGHT EVEN HAVE DIVINE POWERS OR . . .
TSK, TSK! WOMEN TODAY JUST DON'T KNOW THEIR *PLACE.*
WHAT'S *SHE* DOING HERE?

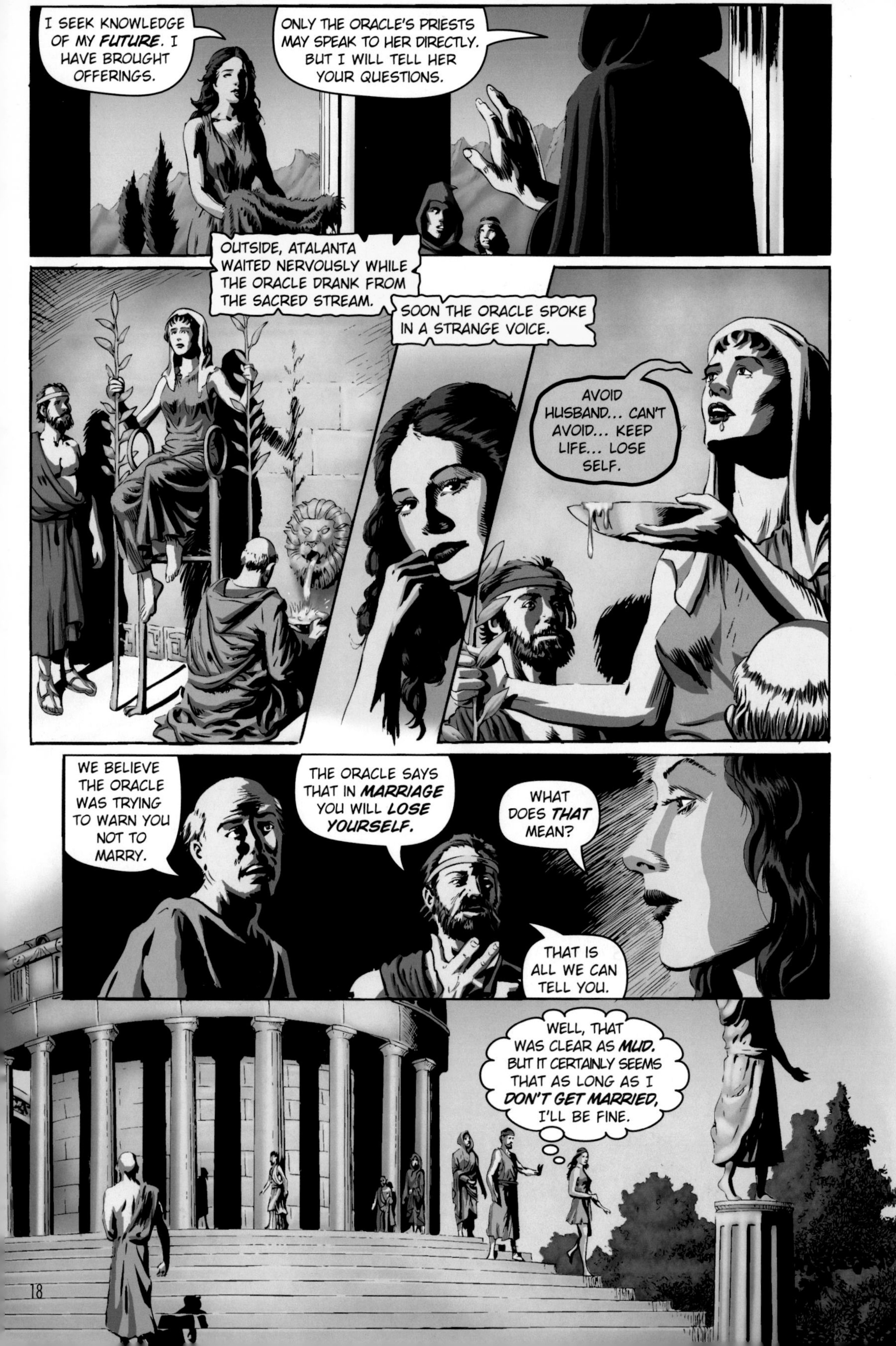
I SEEK KNOWLEDGE OF MY ***FUTURE***. I HAVE BROUGHT OFFERINGS.
ONLY THE ORACLE'S PRIESTS MAY SPEAK TO HER DIRECTLY. BUT I WILL TELL HER YOUR QUESTIONS.
OUTSIDE, ATALANTA WAITED NERVOUSLY WHILE THE ORACLE DRANK FROM THE SACRED STREAM.
SOON THE ORACLE SPOKE IN A STRANGE VOICE.
AVOID HUSBAND... CAN'T AVOID... KEEP LIFE... LOSE SELF.
WE BELIEVE THE ORACLE WAS TRYING TO WARN YOU NOT TO MARRY.
THE ORACLE SAYS THAT IN ***MARRIAGE*** YOU WILL ***LOSE YOURSELF.***
WHAT DOES ***THAT*** MEAN?
THAT IS ALL WE CAN TELL YOU.
WELL, THAT WAS CLEAR AS ***MUD.*** BUT IT CERTAINLY SEEMS THAT AS LONG AS I ***DON'T GET MARRIED,*** I'LL BE FINE.

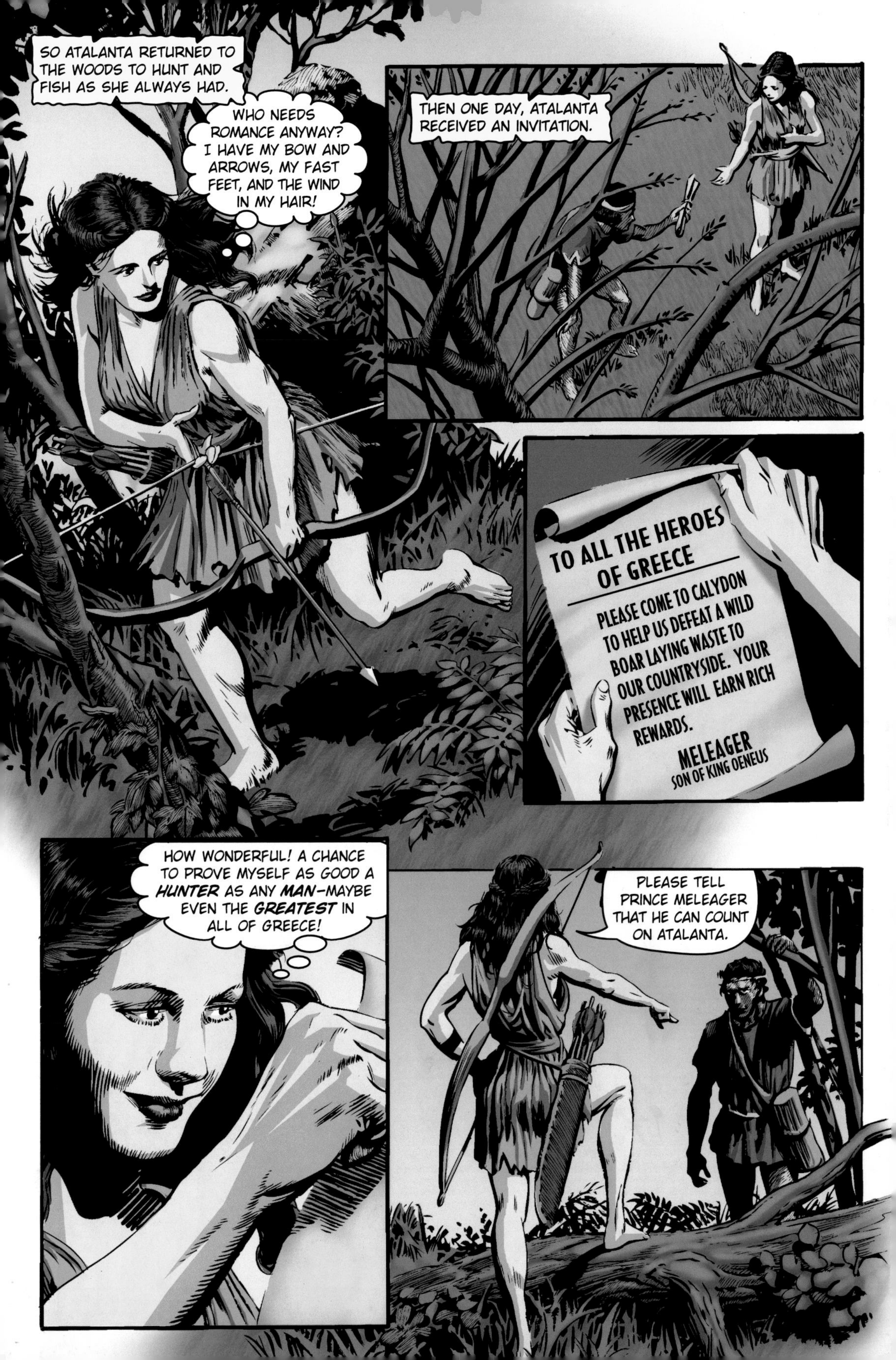
SO ATALANTA RETURNED TO THE WOODS TO HUNT AND FISH AS SHE ALWAYS HAD.
WHO NEEDS ROMANCE ANYWAY? I HAVE MY BOW AND ARROWS, MY FAST FEET, AND THE WIND IN MY HAIR!
THEN ONE DAY, ATALANTA RECEIVED AN INVITATION.
TO ALL THE HEROES OF GREECE
PLEASE COME TO CALYDON TO HELP US DEFEAT A WILD BOAR LAYING WASTE TO OUR COUNTRYSIDE. YOUR PRESENCE WILL EARN RICH REWARDS.
MELEAGER
SON OF KING OENEUS
HOW WONDERFUL! A CHANCE TO PROVE MYSELF AS GOOD A HUNTER AS ANY MAN—MAYBE EVEN THE GREATEST IN ALL OF GREECE!
PLEASE TELL PRINCE MELEAGER THAT HE CAN COUNT ON ATALANTA.

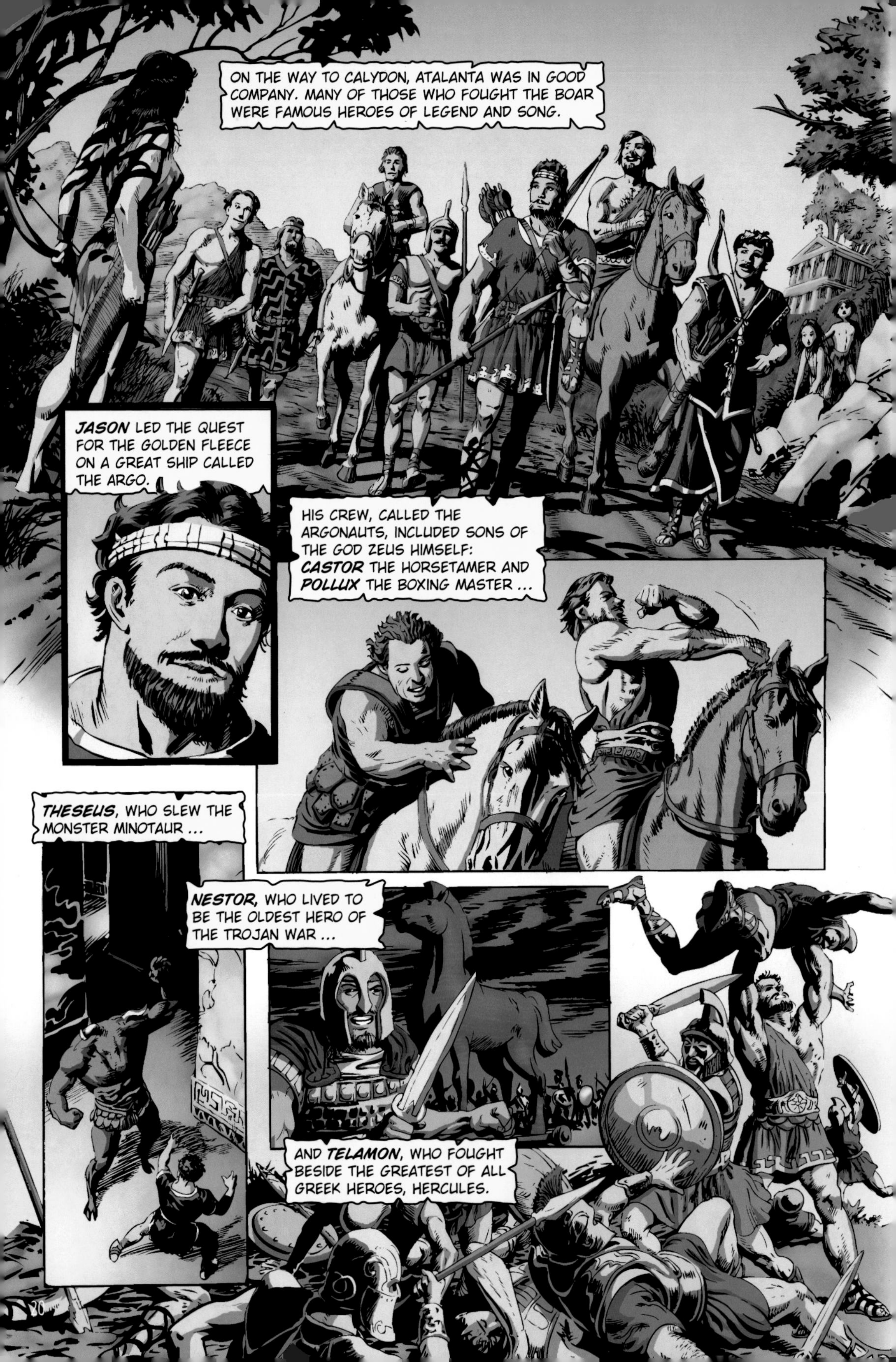
ON THE WAY TO CALYDON, ATALANTA WAS IN GOOD COMPANY. MANY OF THOSE WHO FOUGHT THE BOAR WERE FAMOUS HEROES OF LEGEND AND SONG.
JASON LED THE QUEST FOR THE GOLDEN FLEECE ON A GREAT SHIP CALLED THE ARGO.
HIS CREW, CALLED THE ARGONAUTS, INCLUDED SONS OF THE GOD ZEUS HIMSELF: CASTOR THE HORSETAMER AND POLLUX THE BOXING MASTER ...
THESEUS, WHO SLEW THE MONSTER MINOTAUR ...
NESTOR, WHO LIVED TO BE THE OLDEST HERO OF THE TROJAN WAR ...
AND TELAMON, WHO FOUGHT BESIDE THE GREATEST OF ALL GREEK HEROES, HERCULES.

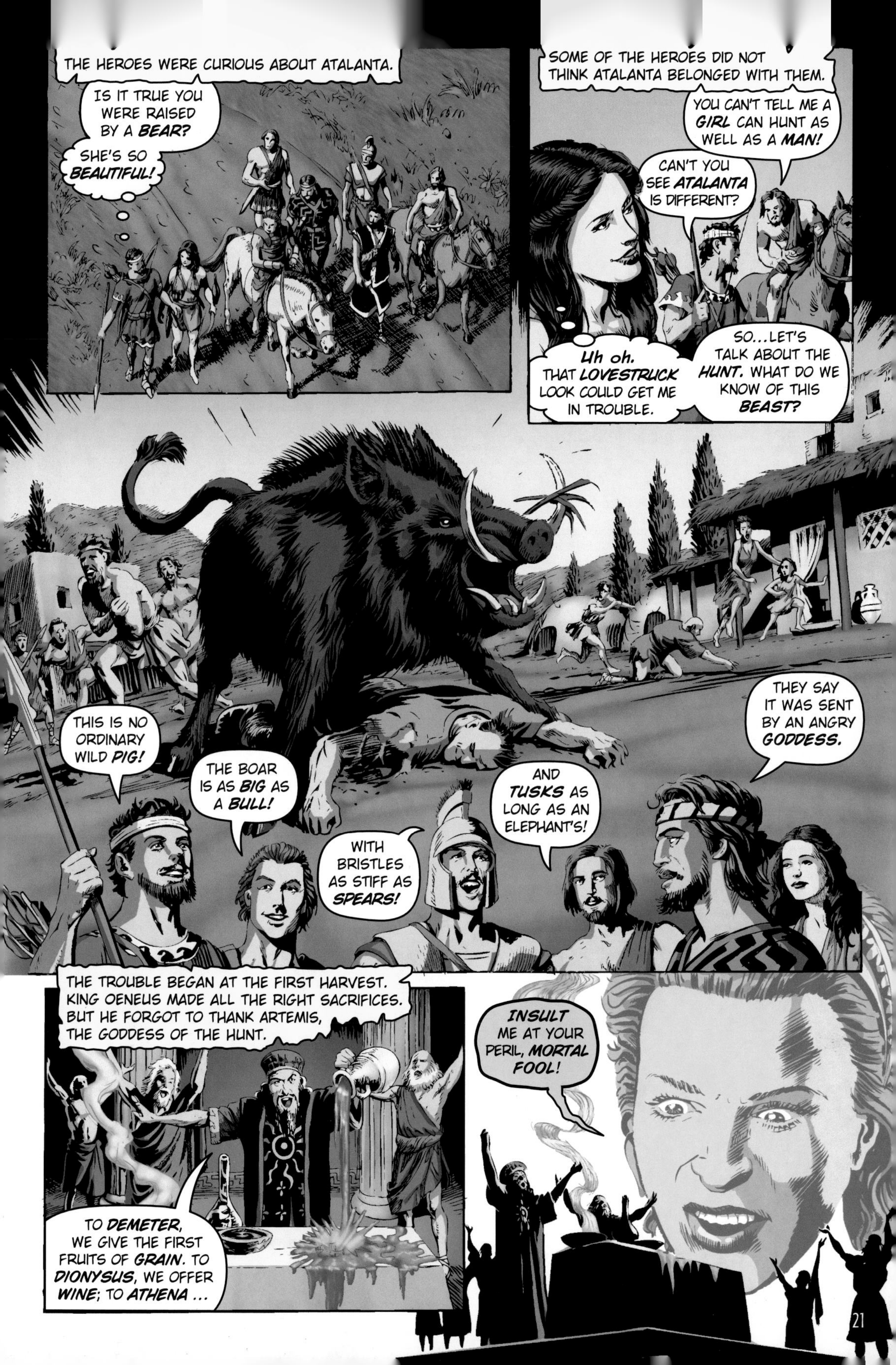
THE HEROES WERE CURIOUS ABOUT ATALANTA.
IS IT TRUE YOU WERE RAISED BY A BEAR?
SHE'S SO BEAUTIFUL!
SOME OF THE HEROES DID NOT THINK ATALANTA BELONGED WITH THEM.
YOU CAN'T TELL ME A GIRL CAN HUNT AS WELL AS A MAN!
CAN'T YOU SEE ATALANTA IS DIFFERENT?
Uh oh. THAT LOVESTRUCK LOOK COULD GET ME IN TROUBLE.
SO...LET'S TALK ABOUT THE HUNT. WHAT DO WE KNOW OF THIS BEAST?
THIS IS NO ORDINARY WILD PIG!
THE BOAR IS AS BIG AS A BULL!
WITH BRISTLES AS STIFF AS SPEARS!
AND TUSKS AS LONG AS AN ELEPHANT'S!
THEY SAY IT WAS SENT BY AN ANGRY GODDESS.
THE TROUBLE BEGAN AT THE FIRST HARVEST. KING OENEUS MADE ALL THE RIGHT SACRIFICES. BUT HE FORGOT TO THANK ARTEMIS, THE GODDESS OF THE HUNT.
TO DEMETER, WE GIVE THE FIRST FRUITS OF GRAIN. TO DIONYSUS, WE OFFER WINE; TO ATHENA ...
INSULT ME AT YOUR PERIL, MORTAL FOOL!

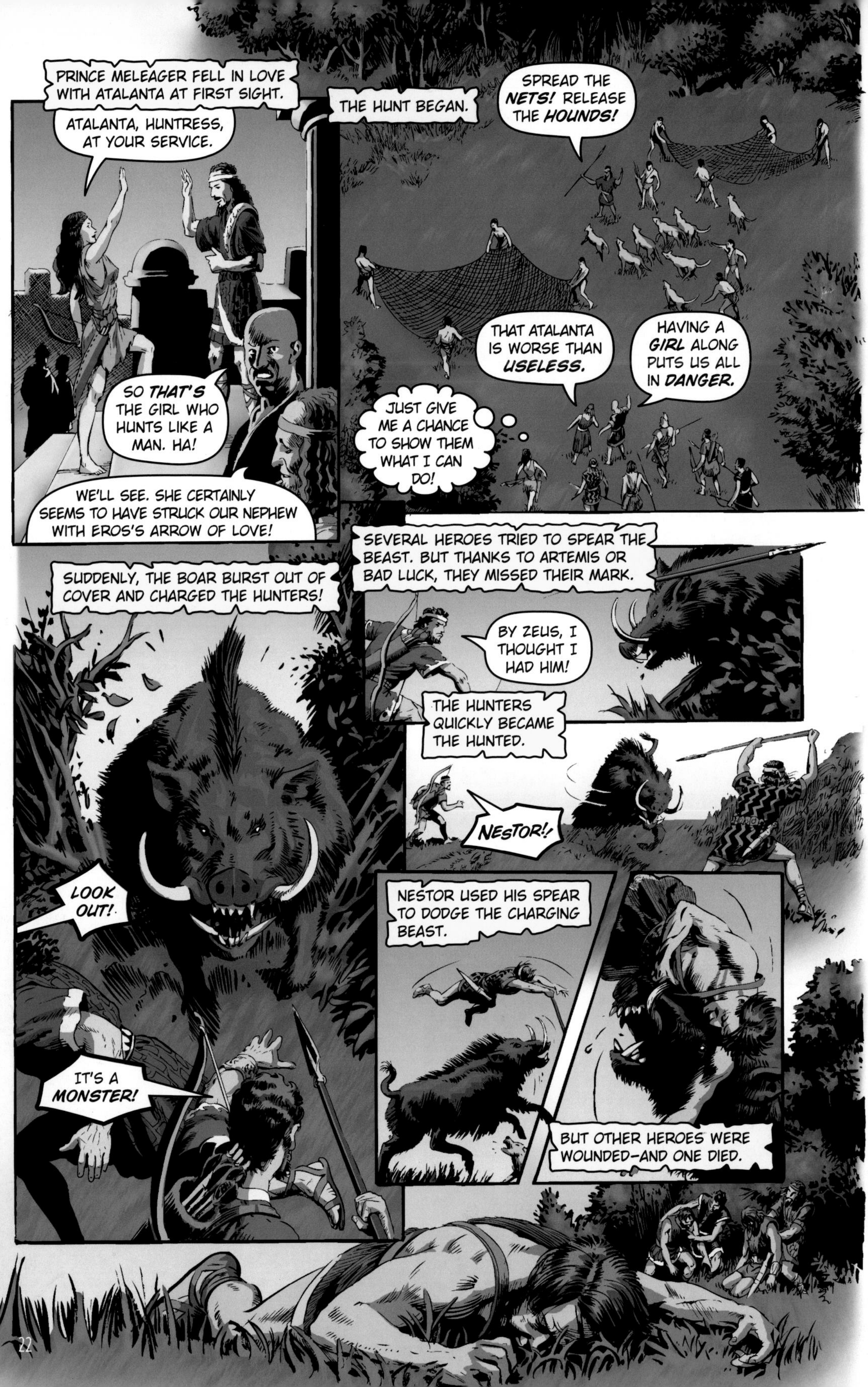
PRINCE MELEAGER FELL IN LOVE WITH ATALANTA AT FIRST SIGHT.
ATALANTA, HUNTRESS, AT YOUR SERVICE.
SO THAT'S THE GIRL WHO HUNTS LIKE A MAN. HA!
WE'LL SEE. SHE CERTAINLY SEEMS TO HAVE STRUCK OUR NEPHEW WITH EROS'S ARROW OF LOVE!
THE HUNT BEGAN.
SPREAD THE NETS! RELEASE THE HOUNDS!
THAT ATALANTA IS WORSE THAN USELESS.
HAVING A GIRL ALONG PUTS US ALL IN DANGER.
JUST GIVE ME A CHANCE TO SHOW THEM WHAT I CAN DO!
SUDDENLY, THE BOAR BURST OUT OF COVER AND CHARGED THE HUNTERS!
LOOK OUT!
IT'S A MONSTER!
SEVERAL HEROES TRIED TO SPEAR THE BEAST. BUT THANKS TO ARTEMIS OR BAD LUCK, THEY MISSED THEIR MARK.
BY ZEUS, I THOUGHT I HAD HIM!
THE HUNTERS QUICKLY BECAME THE HUNTED.
NESTOR!!
NESTOR USED HIS SPEAR TO DODGE THE CHARGING BEAST.
BUT OTHER HEROES WERE WOUNDED—AND ONE DIED.

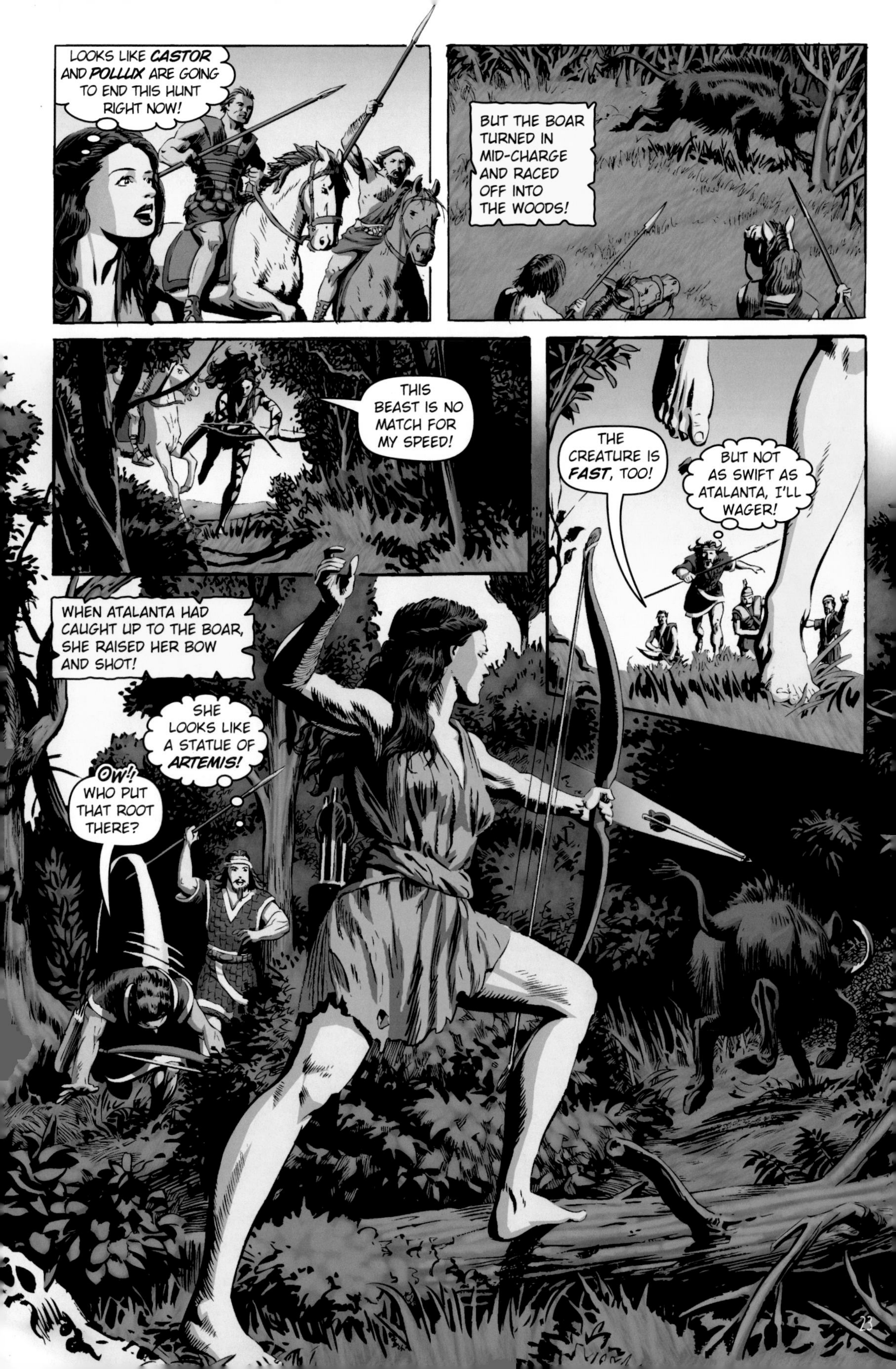
LOOKS LIKE CASTOR AND POLLUX ARE GOING TO END THIS HUNT RIGHT NOW!
BUT THE BOAR TURNED IN MID-CHARGE AND RACED OFF INTO THE WOODS!
THIS BEAST IS NO MATCH FOR MY SPEED!
THE CREATURE IS FAST, TOO!
BUT NOT AS SWIFT AS ATALANTA, I'LL WAGER!
WHEN ATALANTA HAD CAUGHT UP TO THE BOAR, SHE RAISED HER BOW AND SHOT!
SHE LOOKS LIKE A STATUE OF ARTEMIS!
OW!! WHO PUT THAT ROOT THERE?

THWACK!

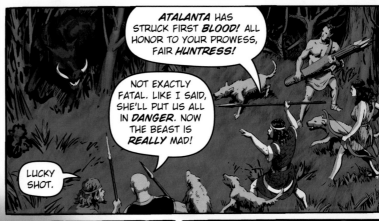

ATALANTA HAS STRUCK FIRST **BLOOD!** ALL HONOR TO YOUR PROWESS, FAIR **HUNTRESS!**

NOT EXACTLY FATAL. LIKE I SAID, SHE'LL PUT US ALL IN **DANGER.** NOW THE BEAST IS **REALLY** MAD!

LUCKY SHOT.

MISSED! BUT NEXT TIME I'LL...

GOT HIM! BUT HE'S NOT DOWN YET...

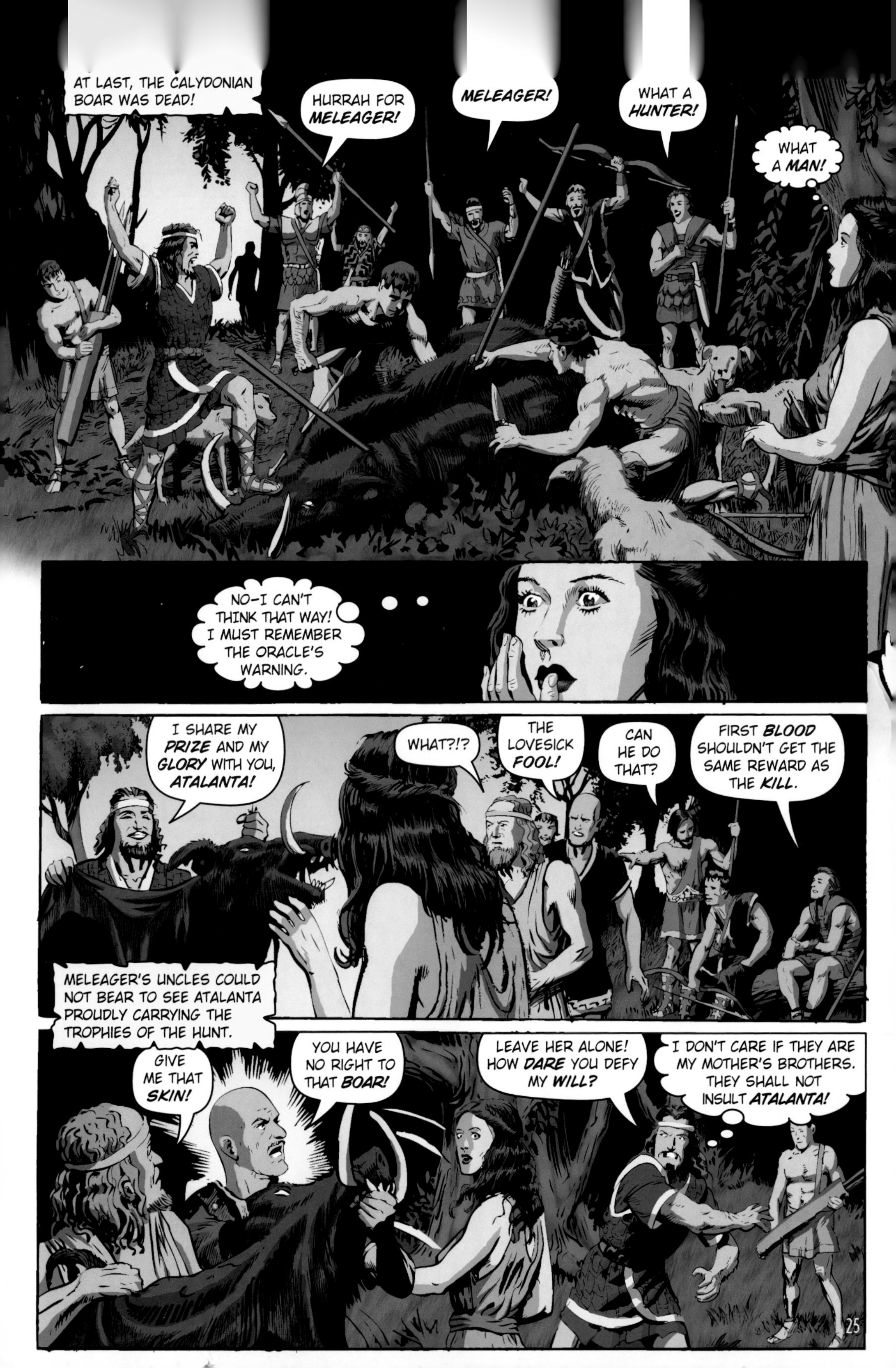

AT LAST, THE CALYDONIAN BOAR WAS DEAD!
HURRAH FOR MELEAGER!
MELEAGER!
WHAT A HUNTER!
WHAT A MAN!
NO—I CAN'T THINK THAT WAY! I MUST REMEMBER THE ORACLE'S WARNING.
I SHARE MY PRIZE AND MY GLORY WITH YOU, ATALANTA!
WHAT?!?
THE LOVESICK FOOL!
CAN HE DO THAT?
FIRST BLOOD SHOULDN'T GET THE SAME REWARD AS THE KILL.
MELEAGER'S UNCLES COULD NOT BEAR TO SEE ATALANTA PROUDLY CARRYING THE TROPHIES OF THE HUNT.
GIVE ME THAT SKIN!
YOU HAVE NO RIGHT TO THAT BOAR!
LEAVE HER ALONE! HOW DARE YOU DEFY MY WILL?
I DON'T CARE IF THEY ARE MY MOTHER'S BROTHERS. THEY SHALL NOT INSULT ATALANTA!

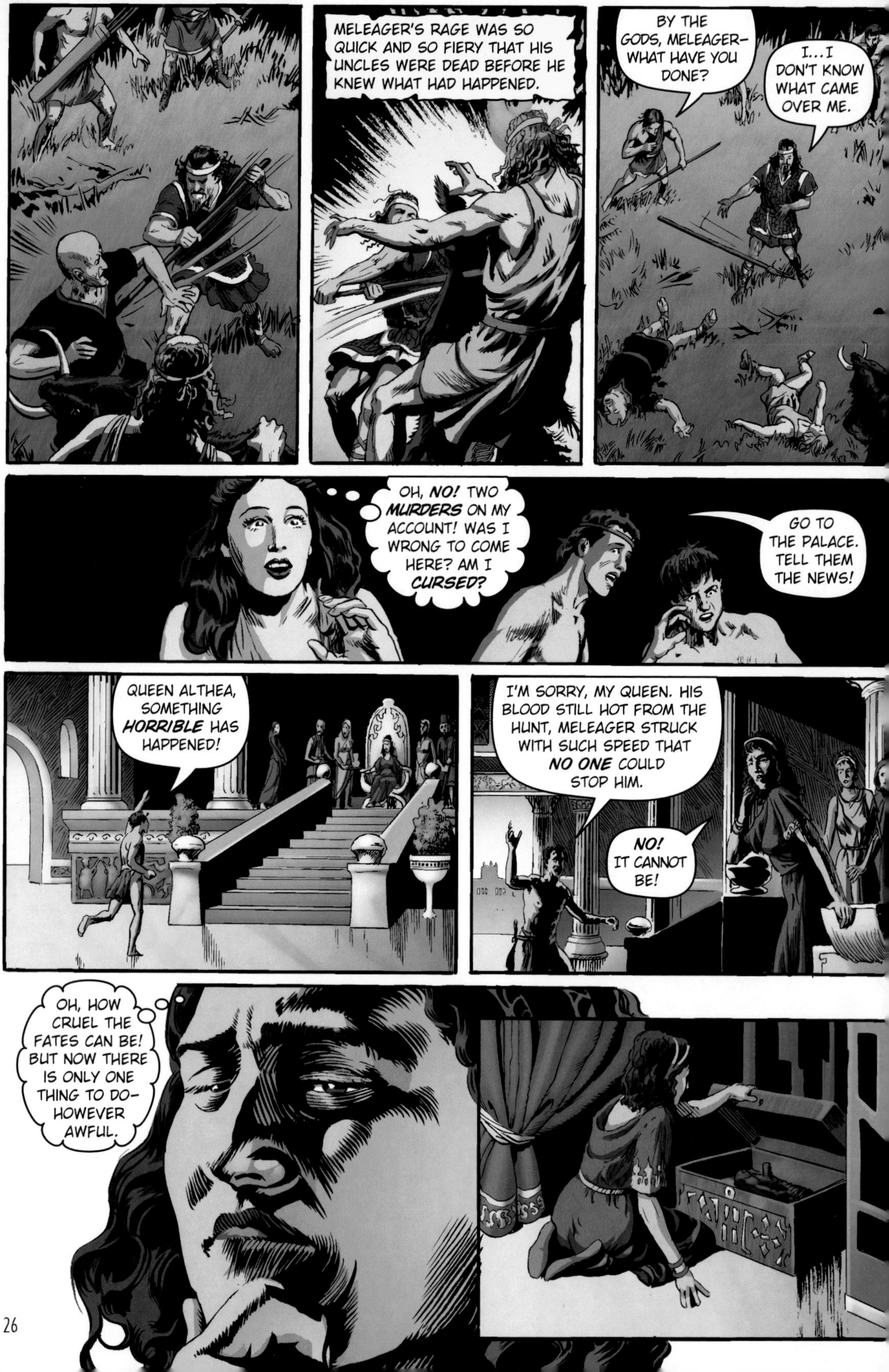

MELEAGER'S RAGE WAS SO QUICK AND SO FIERY THAT HIS UNCLES WERE DEAD BEFORE HE KNEW WHAT HAD HAPPENED.
BY THE GODS, MELEAGER-WHAT HAVE YOU DONE?
I...I DON'T KNOW WHAT CAME OVER ME.
OH, NO! TWO MURDERS ON MY ACCOUNT! WAS I WRONG TO COME HERE? AM I CURSED?
GO TO THE PALACE. TELL THEM THE NEWS!
QUEEN ALTHEA, SOMETHING HORRIBLE HAS HAPPENED!
I'M SORRY, MY QUEEN. HIS BLOOD STILL HOT FROM THE HUNT, MELEAGER STRUCK WITH SUCH SPEED THAT NO ONE COULD STOP HIM.
NO! IT CANNOT BE!
OH, HOW CRUEL THE FATES CAN BE! BUT NOW THERE IS ONLY ONE THING TO DO-HOWEVER AWFUL.

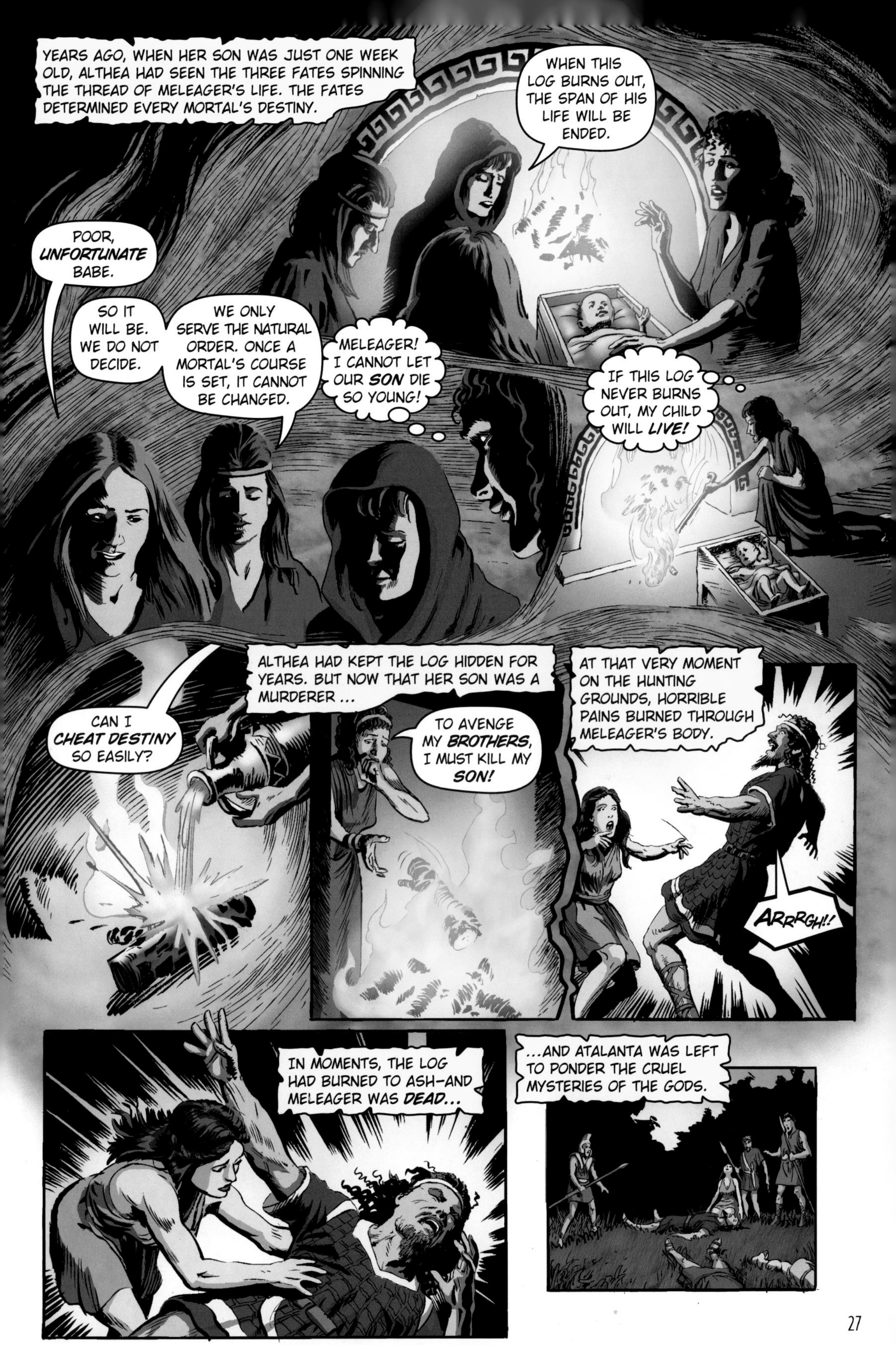
YEARS AGO, WHEN HER SON WAS JUST ONE WEEK OLD, ALTHEA HAD SEEN THE THREE FATES SPINNING THE THREAD OF MELEAGER'S LIFE. THE FATES DETERMINED EVERY MORTAL'S DESTINY.
WHEN THIS LOG BURNS OUT, THE SPAN OF HIS LIFE WILL BE ENDED.
POOR, *UNFORTUNATE* BABE.
SO IT WILL BE. WE DO NOT DECIDE.
WE ONLY SERVE THE NATURAL ORDER. ONCE A MORTAL'S COURSE IS SET, IT CANNOT BE CHANGED.
MELEAGER! I CANNOT LET OUR *SON* DIE SO YOUNG!
IF THIS LOG NEVER BURNS OUT, MY CHILD WILL *LIVE!*
CAN I *CHEAT DESTINY* SO EASILY?
ALTHEA HAD KEPT THE LOG HIDDEN FOR YEARS. BUT NOW THAT HER SON WAS A MURDERER . . .
TO AVENGE MY *BROTHERS*, I MUST KILL MY *SON!*
AT THAT VERY MOMENT ON THE HUNTING GROUNDS, HORRIBLE PAINS BURNED THROUGH MELEAGER'S BODY.
ARRRGH!!
IN MOMENTS, THE LOG HAD BURNED TO ASH—AND MELEAGER WAS *DEAD* . . .
. . . AND ATALANTA WAS LEFT TO PONDER THE CRUEL MYSTERIES OF THE GODS.

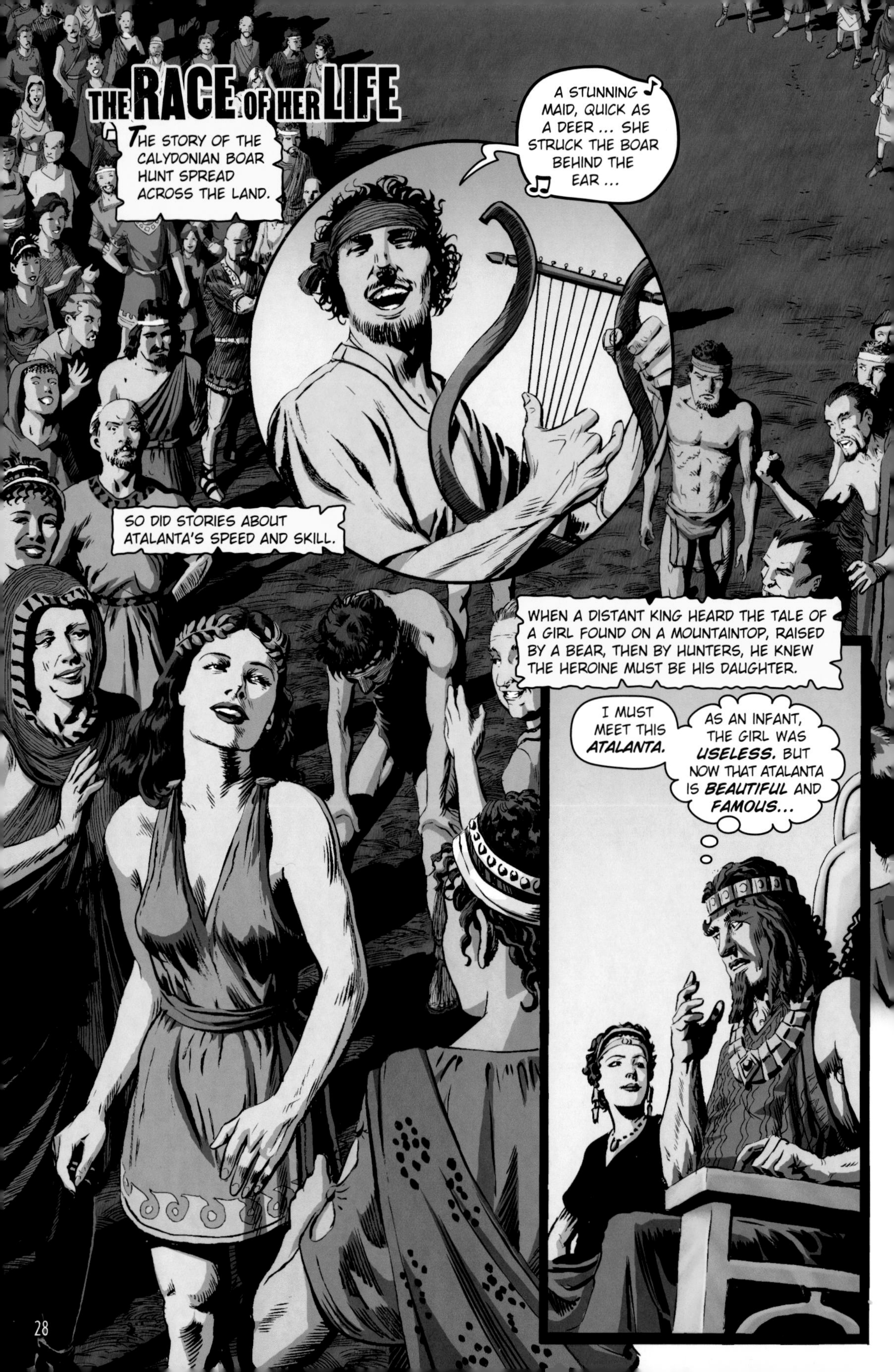

THE RACE OF HER LIFE
THE STORY OF THE CALYDONIAN BOAR HUNT SPREAD ACROSS THE LAND.
A STUNNING MAID, QUICK AS A DEER ... SHE STRUCK THE BOAR BEHIND THE EAR ...
SO DID STORIES ABOUT ATALANTA'S SPEED AND SKILL.
WHEN A DISTANT KING HEARD THE TALE OF A GIRL FOUND ON A MOUNTAINTOP, RAISED BY A BEAR, THEN BY HUNTERS, HE KNEW THE HEROINE MUST BE HIS DAUGHTER.
I MUST MEET THIS ATALANTA.
AS AN INFANT, THE GIRL WAS USELESS. BUT NOW THAT ATALANTA IS BEAUTIFUL AND FAMOUS...

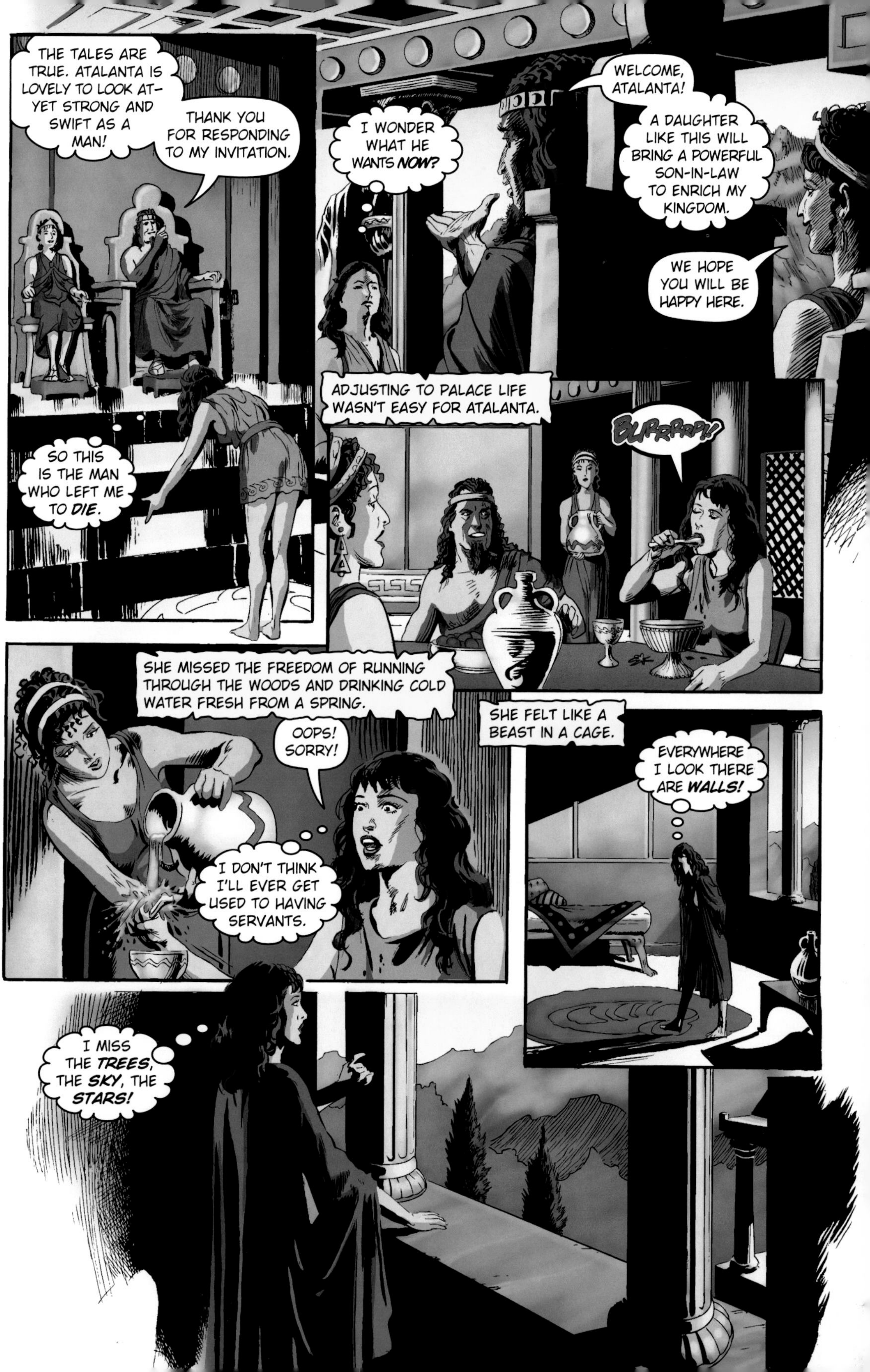
THE TALES ARE TRUE. ATALANTA IS LOVELY TO LOOK AT- YET STRONG AND SWIFT AS A MAN!
THANK YOU FOR RESPONDING TO MY INVITATION.
SO THIS IS THE MAN WHO LEFT ME TO DIE.
I WONDER WHAT HE WANTS NOW?
WELCOME, ATALANTA!
A DAUGHTER LIKE THIS WILL BRING A POWERFUL SON-IN-LAW TO ENRICH MY KINGDOM.
WE HOPE YOU WILL BE HAPPY HERE.
ADJUSTING TO PALACE LIFE WASN'T EASY FOR ATALANTA.
BURRRRP!
SHE MISSED THE FREEDOM OF RUNNING THROUGH THE WOODS AND DRINKING COLD WATER FRESH FROM A SPRING.
OOPS! SORRY!
I DON'T THINK I'LL EVER GET USED TO HAVING SERVANTS.
SHE FELT LIKE A BEAST IN A CAGE.
EVERYWHERE I LOOK THERE ARE WALLS!
I MISS THE TREES, THE SKY, THE STARS!

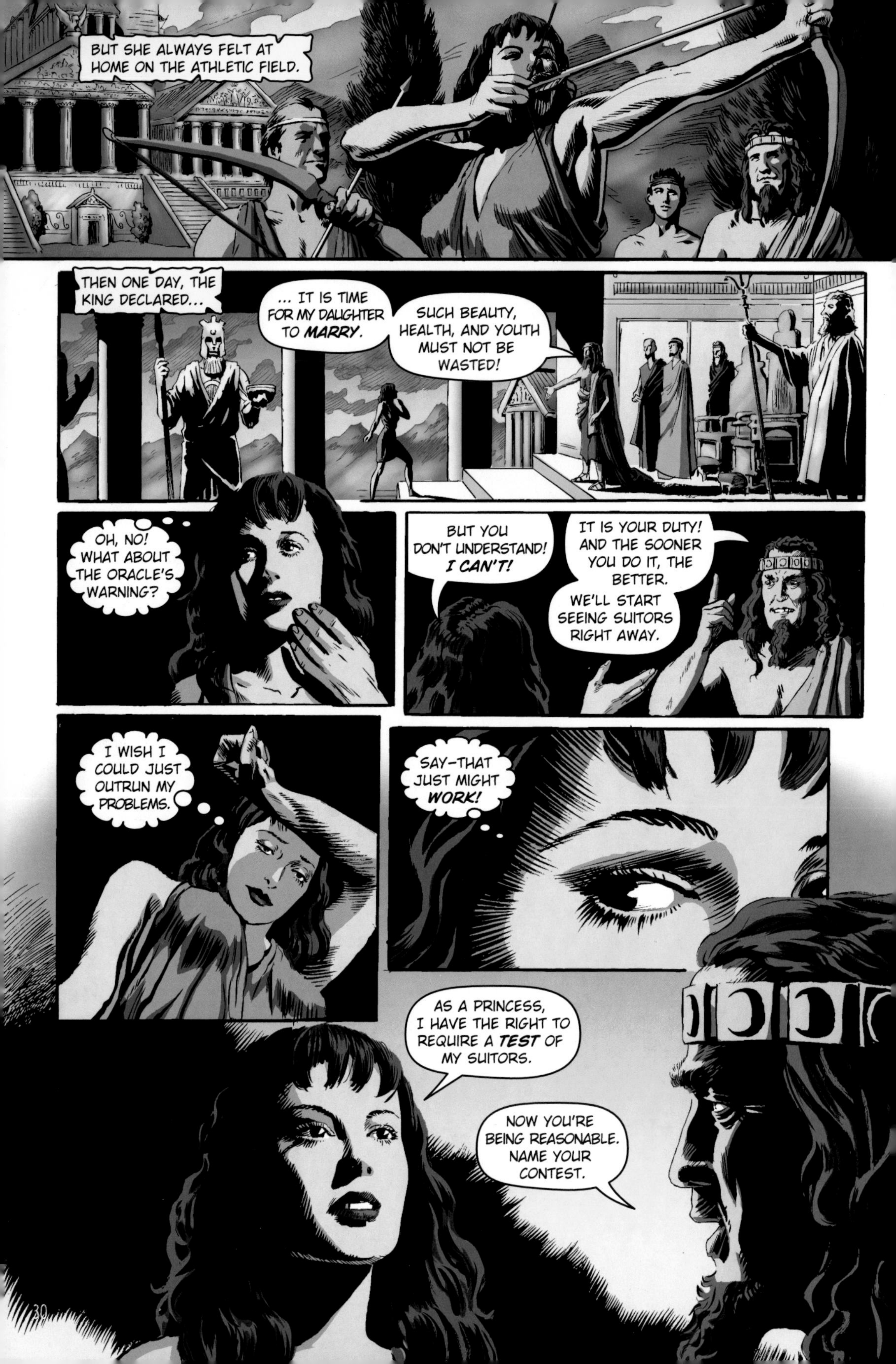
BUT SHE ALWAYS FELT AT HOME ON THE ATHLETIC FIELD.
THEN ONE DAY, THE KING DECLARED...
... IT IS TIME FOR MY DAUGHTER TO MARRY.
SUCH BEAUTY, HEALTH, AND YOUTH MUST NOT BE WASTED!
OH, NO! WHAT ABOUT THE ORACLE'S WARNING?
BUT YOU DON'T UNDERSTAND! I CAN'T!
IT IS YOUR DUTY! AND THE SOONER YOU DO IT, THE BETTER.
WE'LL START SEEING SUITORS RIGHT AWAY.
I WISH I COULD JUST OUTRUN MY PROBLEMS.
SAY—THAT JUST MIGHT WORK!
AS A PRINCESS, I HAVE THE RIGHT TO REQUIRE A TEST OF MY SUITORS.
NOW YOU'RE BEING REASONABLE. NAME YOUR CONTEST.

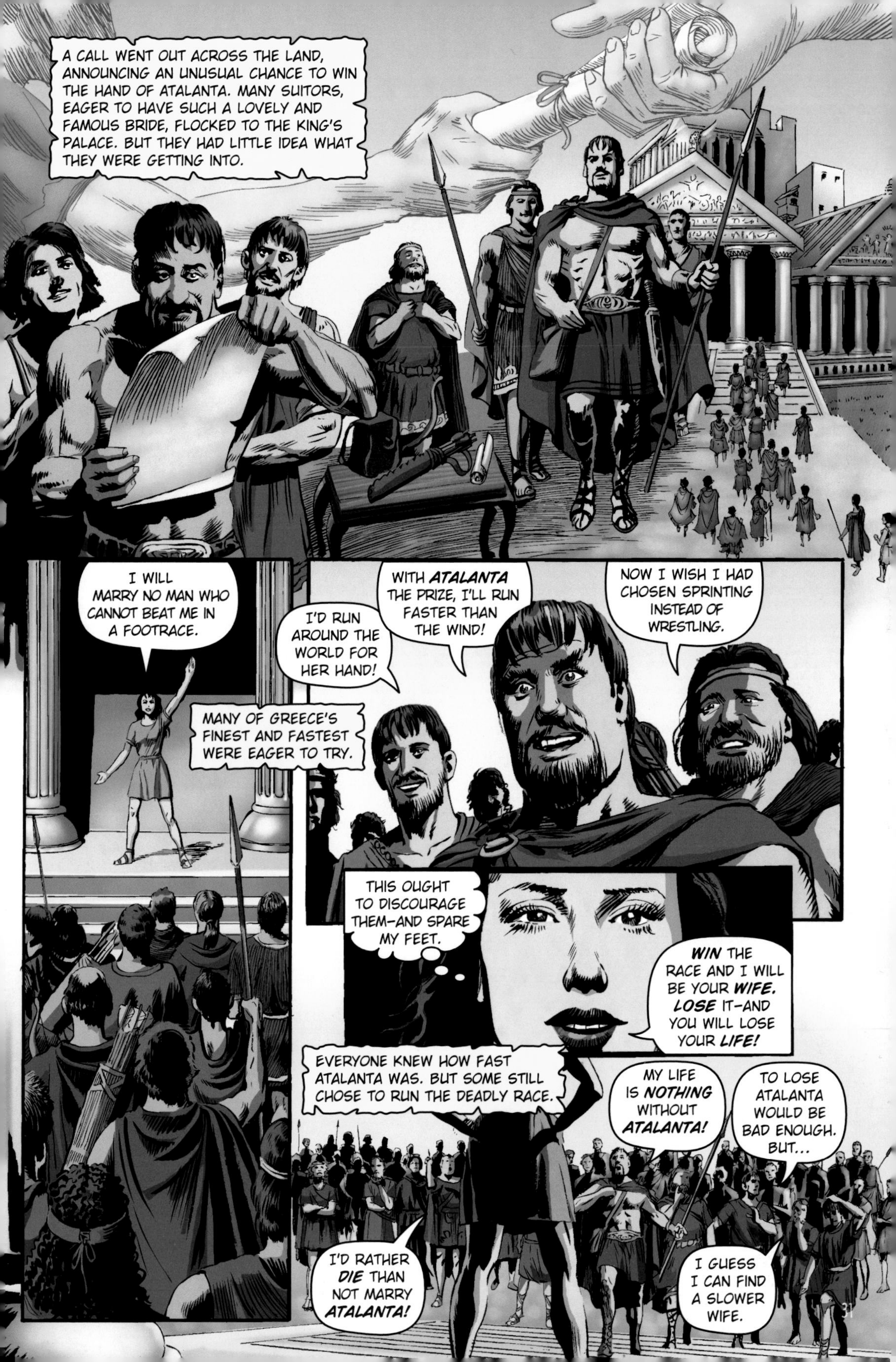

A CALL WENT OUT ACROSS THE LAND, ANNOUNCING AN UNUSUAL CHANCE TO WIN THE HAND OF ATALANTA. MANY SUITORS, EAGER TO HAVE SUCH A LOVELY AND FAMOUS BRIDE, FLOCKED TO THE KING'S PALACE. BUT THEY HAD LITTLE IDEA WHAT THEY WERE GETTING INTO.
I WILL MARRY NO MAN WHO CANNOT BEAT ME IN A FOOTRACE.
MANY OF GREECE'S FINEST AND FASTEST WERE EAGER TO TRY.
I'D RUN AROUND THE WORLD FOR HER HAND!
WITH ATALANTA THE PRIZE, I'LL RUN FASTER THAN THE WIND!
NOW I WISH I HAD CHOSEN SPRINTING INSTEAD OF WRESTLING.
THIS OUGHT TO DISCOURAGE THEM—AND SPARE MY FEET.
WIN THE RACE AND I WILL BE YOUR WIFE. LOSE IT—AND YOU WILL LOSE YOUR LIFE!
EVERYONE KNEW HOW FAST ATALANTA WAS. BUT SOME STILL CHOSE TO RUN THE DEADLY RACE.
MY LIFE IS NOTHING WITHOUT ATALANTA!
TO LOSE ATALANTA WOULD BE BAD ENOUGH. BUT...
I'D RATHER DIE THAN NOT MARRY ATALANTA!
I GUESS I CAN FIND A SLOWER WIFE.

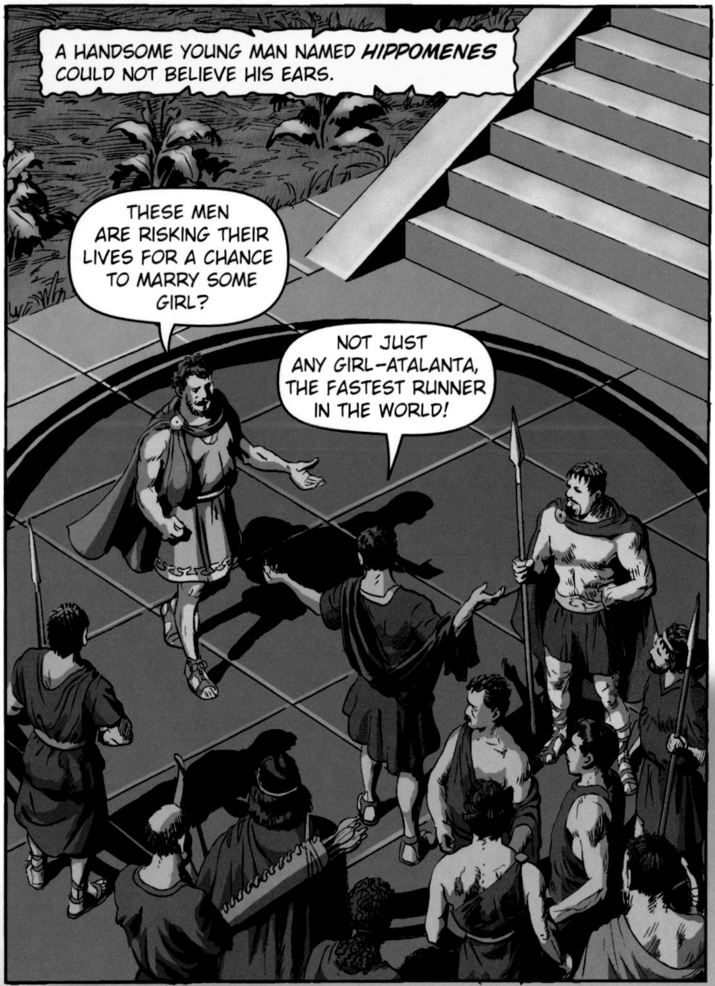
A HANDSOME YOUNG MAN NAMED **HIPPOMENES** COULD NOT BELIEVE HIS EARS.
THESE MEN ARE RISKING THEIR LIVES FOR A CHANCE TO MARRY SOME GIRL?
NOT JUST ANY GIRL—ATALANTA, THE FASTEST RUNNER IN THE WORLD!

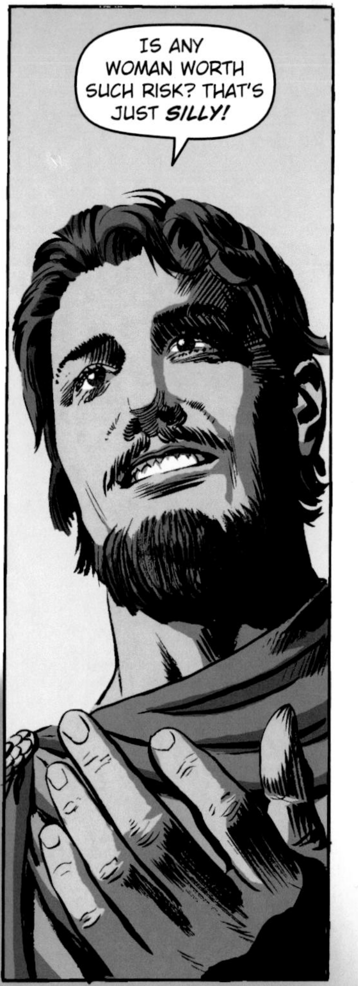
IS ANY WOMAN WORTH SUCH RISK? THAT'S JUST **SILLY!**

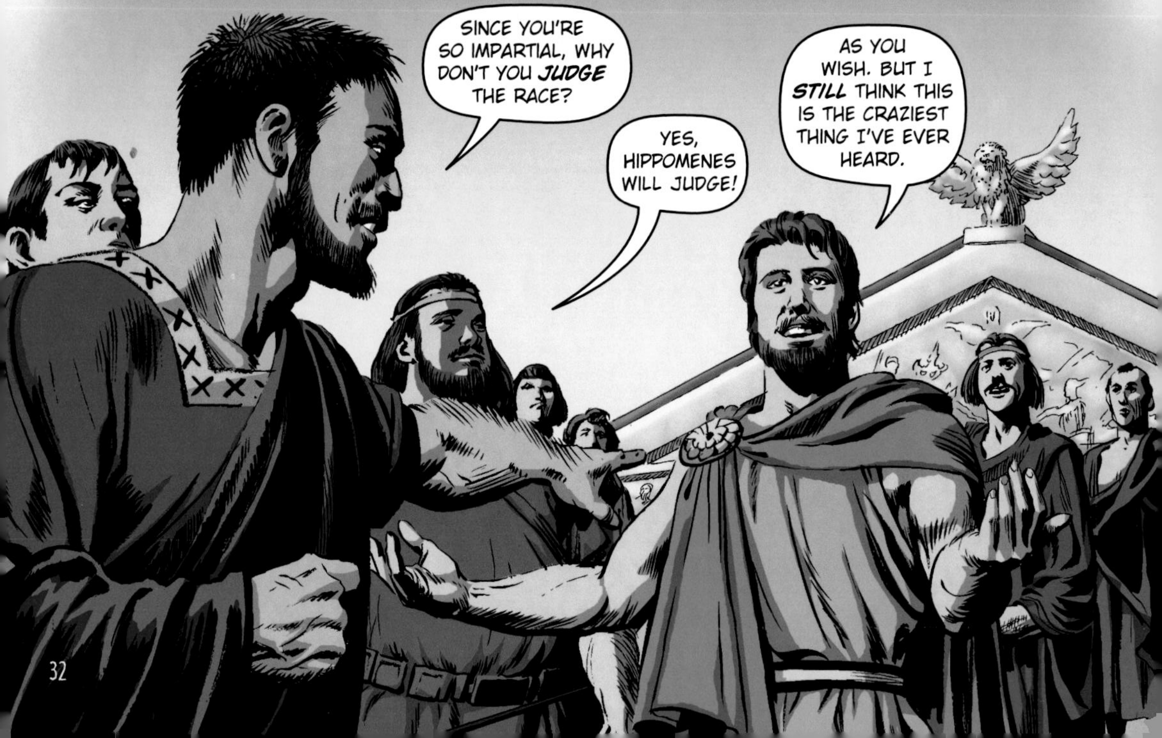
SINCE YOU'RE SO IMPARTIAL, WHY DON'T YOU **JUDGE** THE RACE?
YES, HIPPOMENES WILL JUDGE!
AS YOU WISH. BUT I **STILL** THINK THIS IS THE CRAZIEST THING I'VE EVER HEARD.

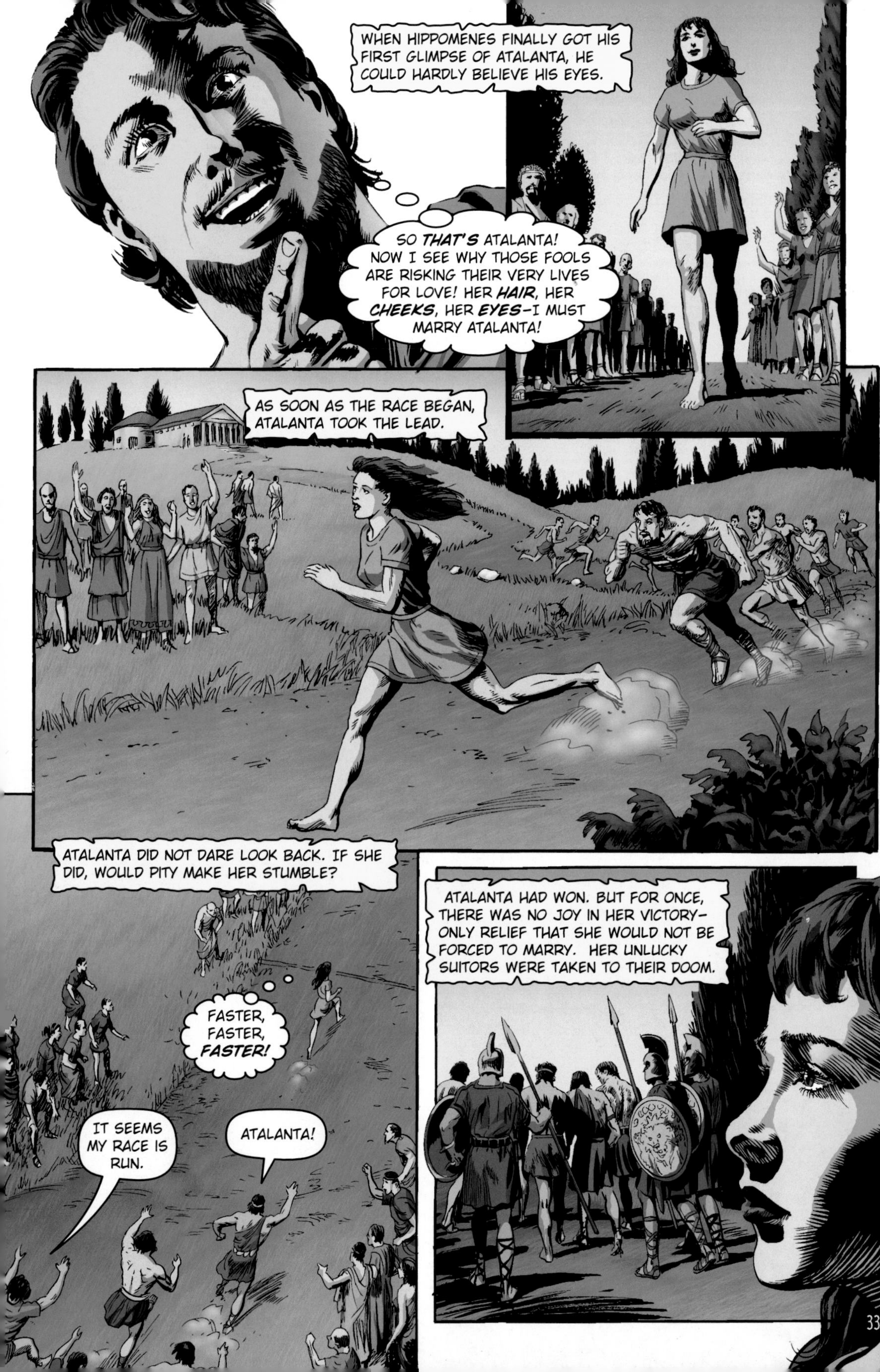

WHEN HIPPOMENES FINALLY GOT HIS FIRST GLIMPSE OF ATALANTA, HE COULD HARDLY BELIEVE HIS EYES.
SO THAT'S ATALANTA! NOW I SEE WHY THOSE FOOLS ARE RISKING THEIR VERY LIVES FOR LOVE! HER HAIR, HER CHEEKS, HER EYES–I MUST MARRY ATALANTA!
AS SOON AS THE RACE BEGAN, ATALANTA TOOK THE LEAD.
ATALANTA DID NOT DARE LOOK BACK. IF SHE DID, WOULD PITY MAKE HER STUMBLE?
FASTER, FASTER, FASTER!
IT SEEMS MY RACE IS RUN.
ATALANTA!
ATALANTA HAD WON. BUT FOR ONCE, THERE WAS NO JOY IN HER VICTORY–ONLY RELIEF THAT SHE WOULD NOT BE FORCED TO MARRY. HER UNLUCKY SUITORS WERE TAKEN TO THEIR DOOM.

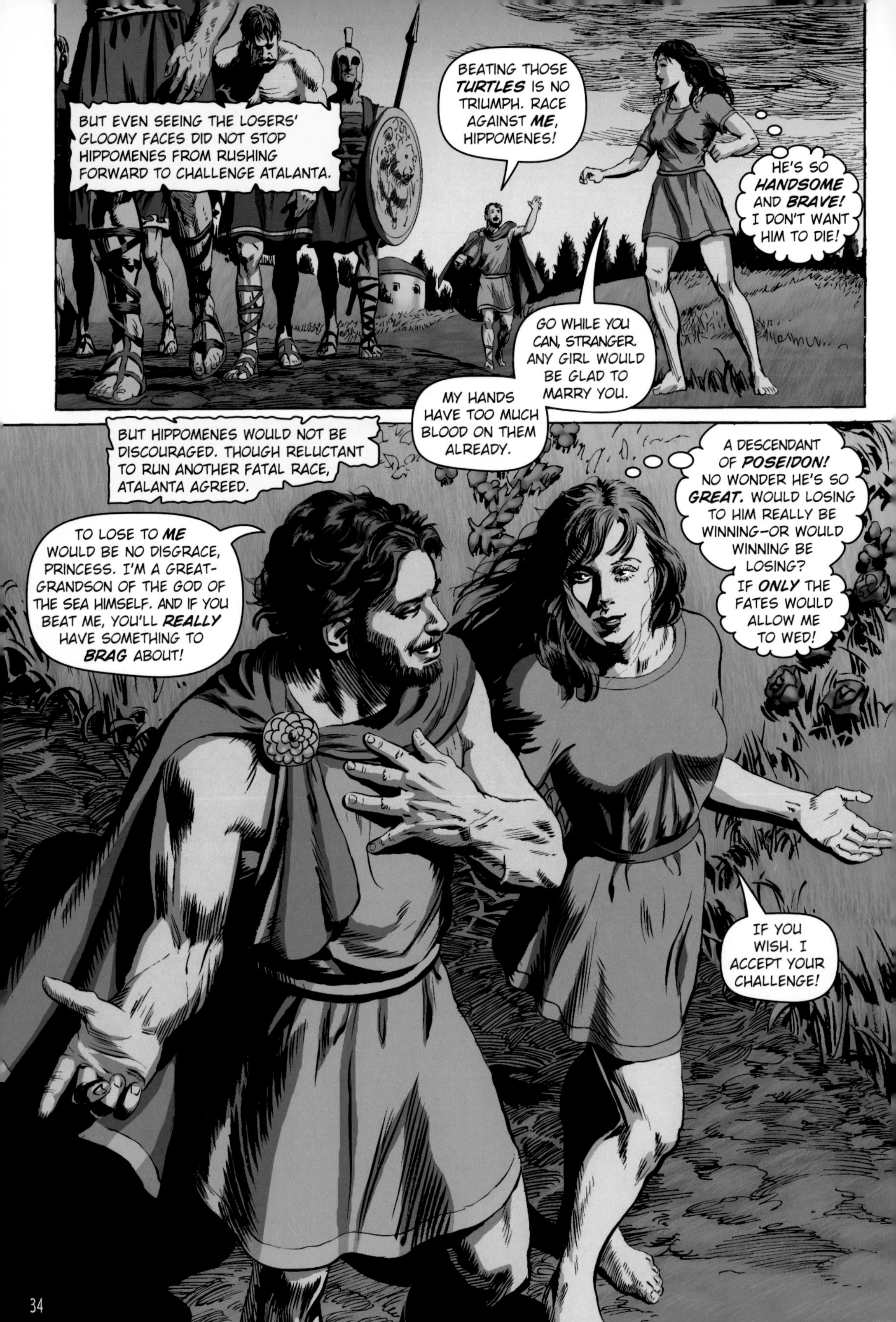
BUT EVEN SEEING THE LOSERS' GLOOMY FACES DID NOT STOP HIPPOMENES FROM RUSHING FORWARD TO CHALLENGE ATALANTA.
BEATING THOSE TURTLES IS NO TRIUMPH. RACE AGAINST ME, HIPPOMENES!
HE'S SO HANDSOME AND BRAVE! I DON'T WANT HIM TO DIE!
GO WHILE YOU CAN, STRANGER. ANY GIRL WOULD BE GLAD TO MARRY YOU.
MY HANDS HAVE TOO MUCH BLOOD ON THEM ALREADY.
BUT HIPPOMENES WOULD NOT BE DISCOURAGED. THOUGH RELUCTANT TO RUN ANOTHER FATAL RACE, ATALANTA AGREED.
TO LOSE TO ME WOULD BE NO DISGRACE, PRINCESS. I'M A GREAT-GRANDSON OF THE GOD OF THE SEA HIMSELF. AND IF YOU BEAT ME, YOU'LL REALLY HAVE SOMETHING TO BRAG ABOUT!
A DESCENDANT OF POSEIDON! NO WONDER HE'S SO GREAT. WOULD LOSING TO HIM REALLY BE WINNING—OR WOULD WINNING BE LOSING? IF ONLY THE FATES WOULD ALLOW ME TO WED!
IF YOU WISH. I ACCEPT YOUR CHALLENGE!

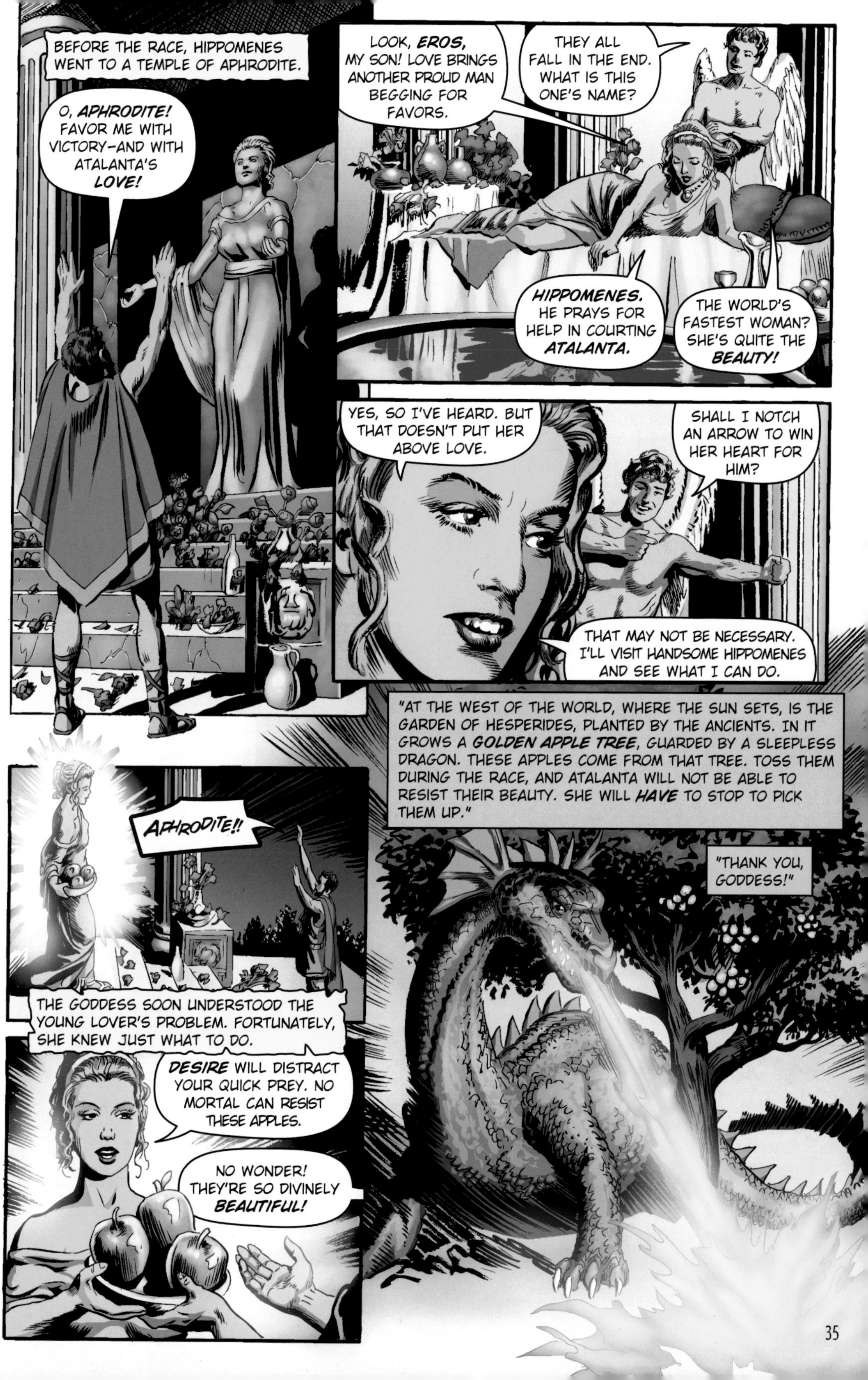
BEFORE THE RACE, HIPPOMENES WENT TO A TEMPLE OF APHRODITE.
O, APHRODITE! FAVOR ME WITH VICTORY—AND WITH ATALANTA'S LOVE!
LOOK, EROS, MY SON! LOVE BRINGS ANOTHER PROUD MAN BEGGING FOR FAVORS.
THEY ALL FALL IN THE END. WHAT IS THIS ONE'S NAME?
HIPPOMENES. HE PRAYS FOR HELP IN COURTING ATALANTA.
THE WORLD'S FASTEST WOMAN? SHE'S QUITE THE BEAUTY!
YES, SO I'VE HEARD. BUT THAT DOESN'T PUT HER ABOVE LOVE.
SHALL I NOTCH AN ARROW TO WIN HER HEART FOR HIM?
THAT MAY NOT BE NECESSARY. I'LL VISIT HANDSOME HIPPOMENES AND SEE WHAT I CAN DO.
APHRODITE!!
THE GODDESS SOON UNDERSTOOD THE YOUNG LOVER'S PROBLEM. FORTUNATELY, SHE KNEW JUST WHAT TO DO.
DESIRE WILL DISTRACT YOUR QUICK PREY. NO MORTAL CAN RESIST THESE APPLES.
NO WONDER! THEY'RE SO DIVINELY BEAUTIFUL!
"AT THE WEST OF THE WORLD, WHERE THE SUN SETS, IS THE GARDEN OF HESPERIDES, PLANTED BY THE ANCIENTS. IN IT GROWS A GOLDEN APPLE TREE, GUARDED BY A SLEEPLESS DRAGON. THESE APPLES COME FROM THAT TREE. TOSS THEM DURING THE RACE, AND ATALANTA WILL NOT BE ABLE TO RESIST THEIR BEAUTY. SHE WILL HAVE TO STOP TO PICK THEM UP."
"THANK YOU, GODDESS!"

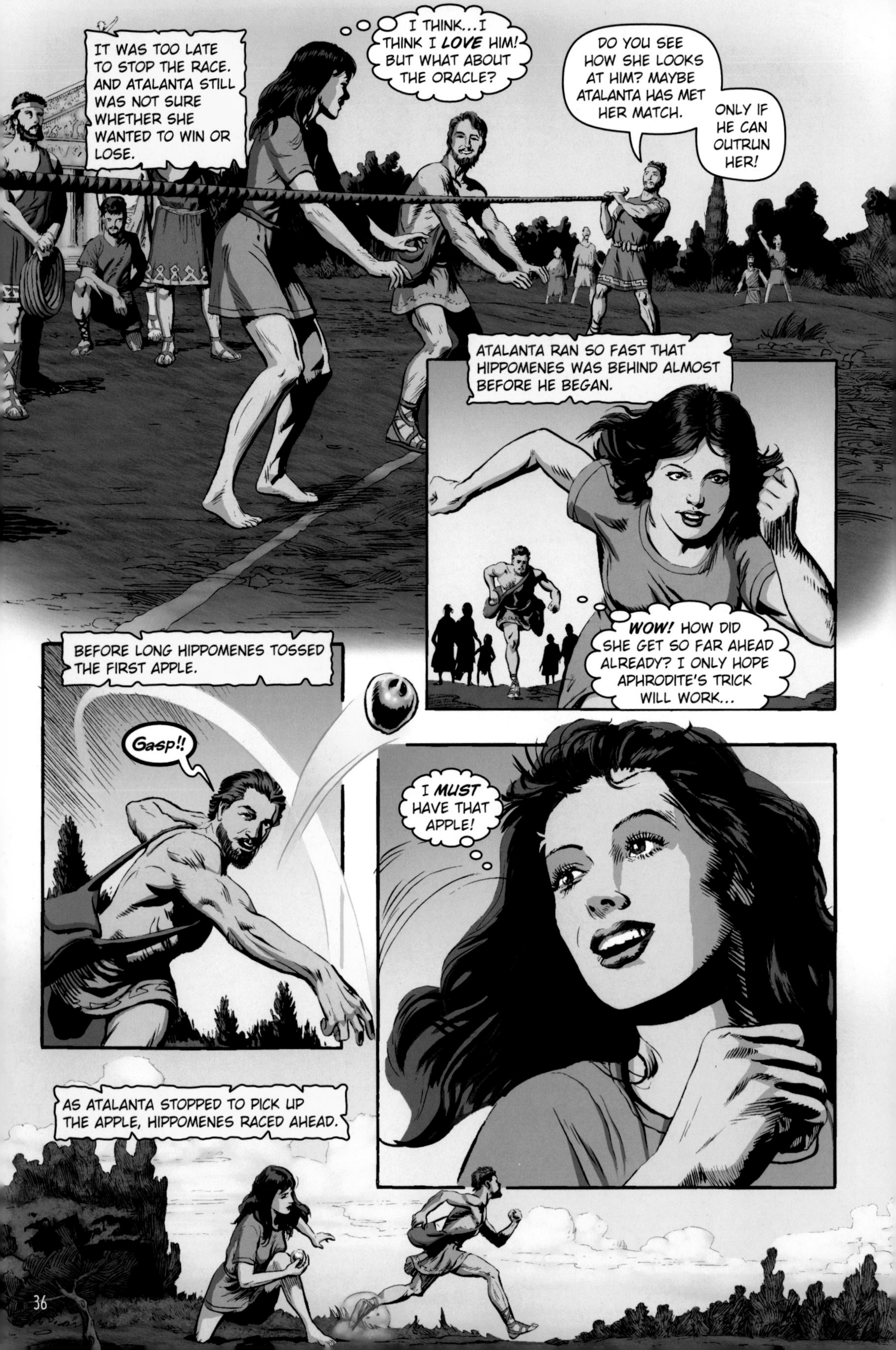

IT WAS TOO LATE TO STOP THE RACE. AND ATALANTA STILL WAS NOT SURE WHETHER SHE WANTED TO WIN OR LOSE.
I THINK...I THINK I LOVE HIM! BUT WHAT ABOUT THE ORACLE?
DO YOU SEE HOW SHE LOOKS AT HIM? MAYBE ATALANTA HAS MET HER MATCH.
ONLY IF HE CAN OUTRUN HER!
ATALANTA RAN SO FAST THAT HIPPOMENES WAS BEHIND ALMOST BEFORE HE BEGAN.
WOW! HOW DID SHE GET SO FAR AHEAD ALREADY? I ONLY HOPE APHRODITE'S TRICK WILL WORK...
BEFORE LONG HIPPOMENES TOSSED THE FIRST APPLE.
Gasp!!
I MUST HAVE THAT APPLE!
AS ATALANTA STOPPED TO PICK UP THE APPLE, HIPPOMENES RACED AHEAD.

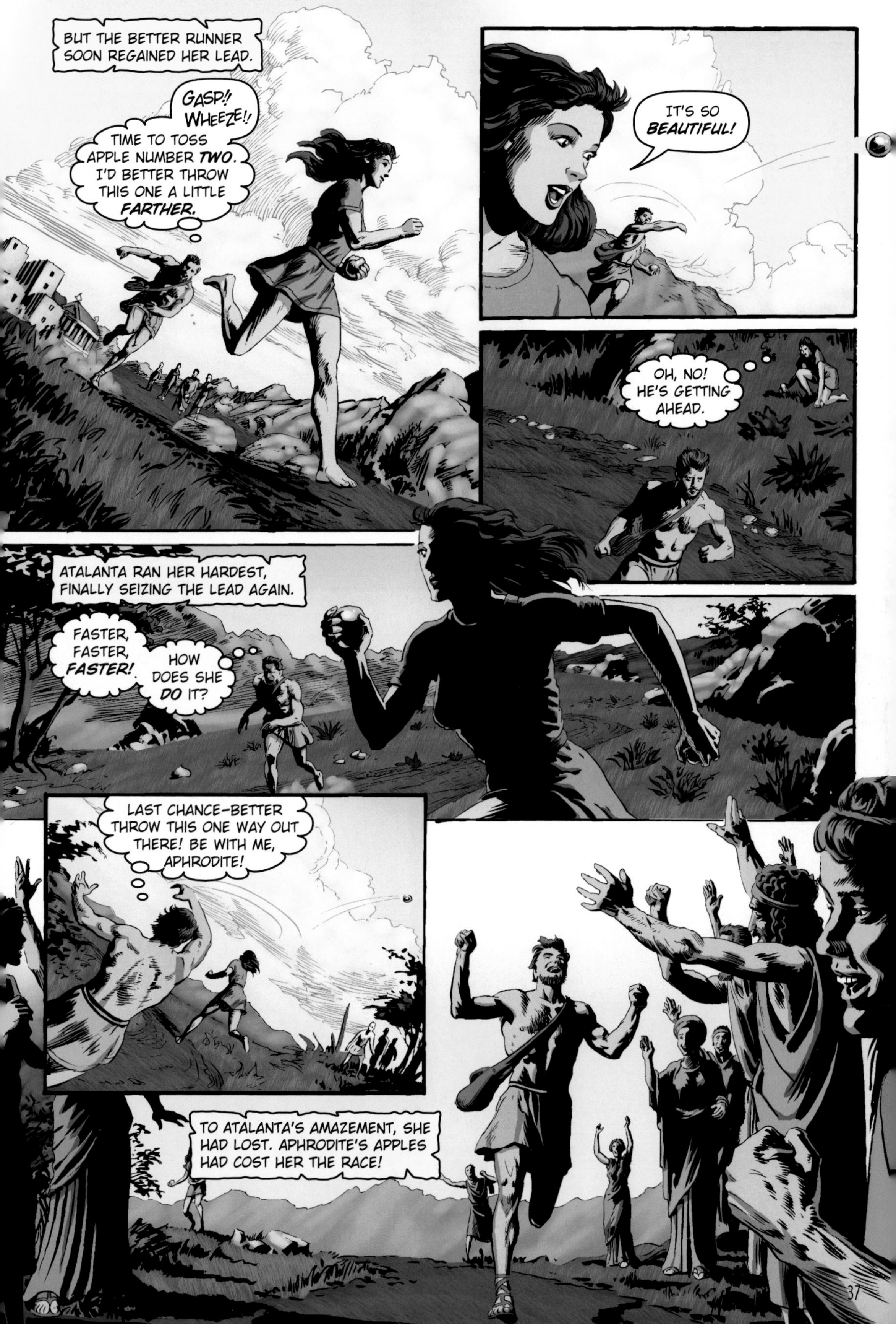
BUT THE BETTER RUNNER SOON REGAINED HER LEAD.
GASP!! WHEEZE!!
TIME TO TOSS APPLE NUMBER TWO. I'D BETTER THROW THIS ONE A LITTLE FARTHER.
IT'S SO BEAUTIFUL!
OH, NO! HE'S GETTING AHEAD.
ATALANTA RAN HER HARDEST, FINALLY SEIZING THE LEAD AGAIN.
FASTER, FASTER, FASTER!
HOW DOES SHE DO IT?
LAST CHANCE—BETTER THROW THIS ONE WAY OUT THERE! BE WITH ME, APHRODITE!
TO ATALANTA'S AMAZEMENT, SHE HAD LOST. APHRODITE'S APPLES HAD COST HER THE RACE!

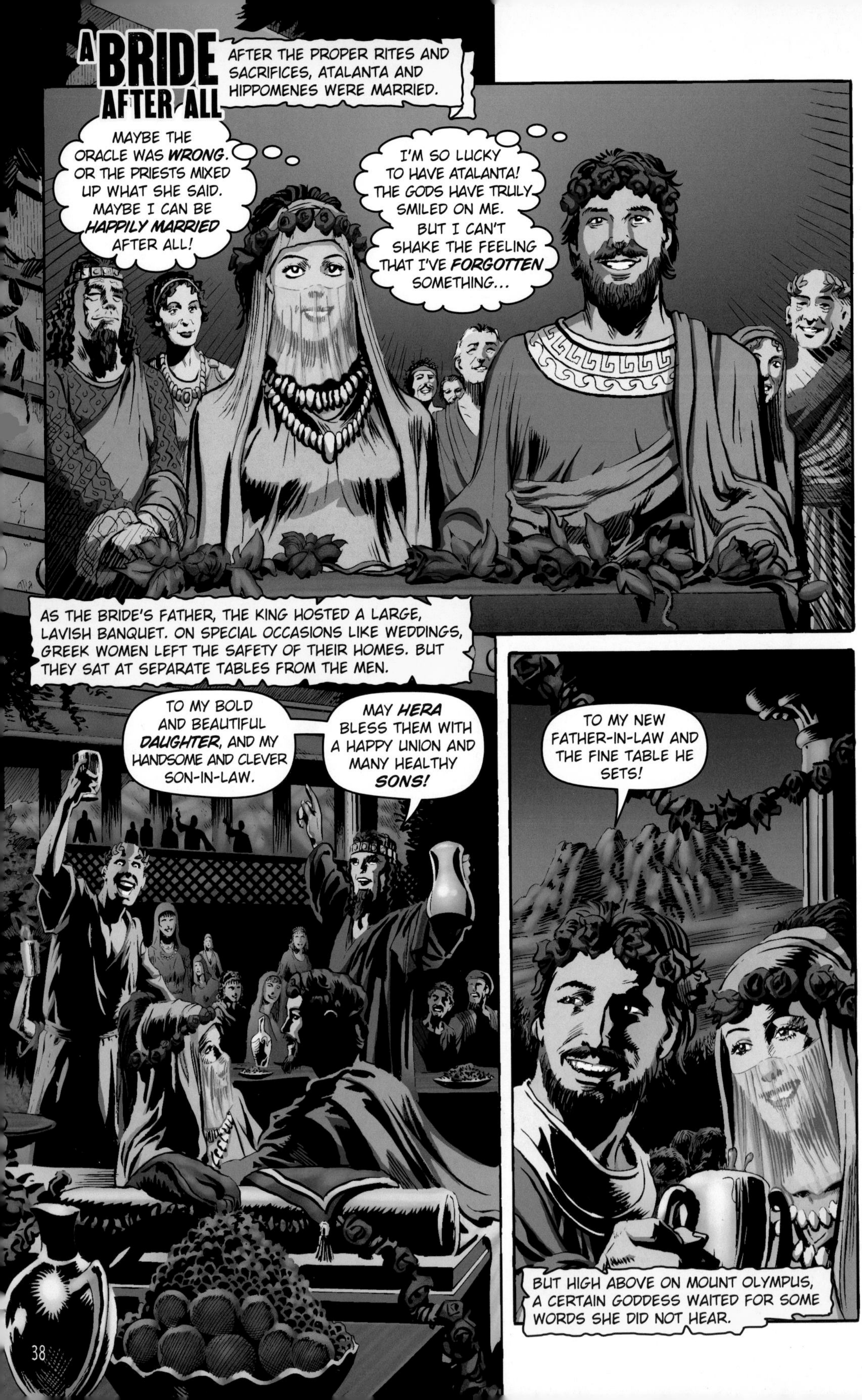
A BRIDE AFTER ALL
AFTER THE PROPER RITES AND SACRIFICES, ATALANTA AND HIPPOMENES WERE MARRIED.
MAYBE THE ORACLE WAS WRONG. OR THE PRIESTS MIXED UP WHAT SHE SAID. MAYBE I CAN BE HAPPILY MARRIED AFTER ALL!
I'M SO LUCKY TO HAVE ATALANTA! THE GODS HAVE TRULY SMILED ON ME. BUT I CAN'T SHAKE THE FEELING THAT I'VE FORGOTTEN SOMETHING...
AS THE BRIDE'S FATHER, THE KING HOSTED A LARGE, LAVISH BANQUET. ON SPECIAL OCCASIONS LIKE WEDDINGS, GREEK WOMEN LEFT THE SAFETY OF THEIR HOMES. BUT THEY SAT AT SEPARATE TABLES FROM THE MEN.
TO MY BOLD AND BEAUTIFUL DAUGHTER, AND MY HANDSOME AND CLEVER SON-IN-LAW.
MAY HERA BLESS THEM WITH A HAPPY UNION AND MANY HEALTHY SONS!
TO MY NEW FATHER-IN-LAW AND THE FINE TABLE HE SETS!
BUT HIGH ABOVE ON MOUNT OLYMPUS, A CERTAIN GODDESS WAITED FOR SOME WORDS SHE DID NOT HEAR.

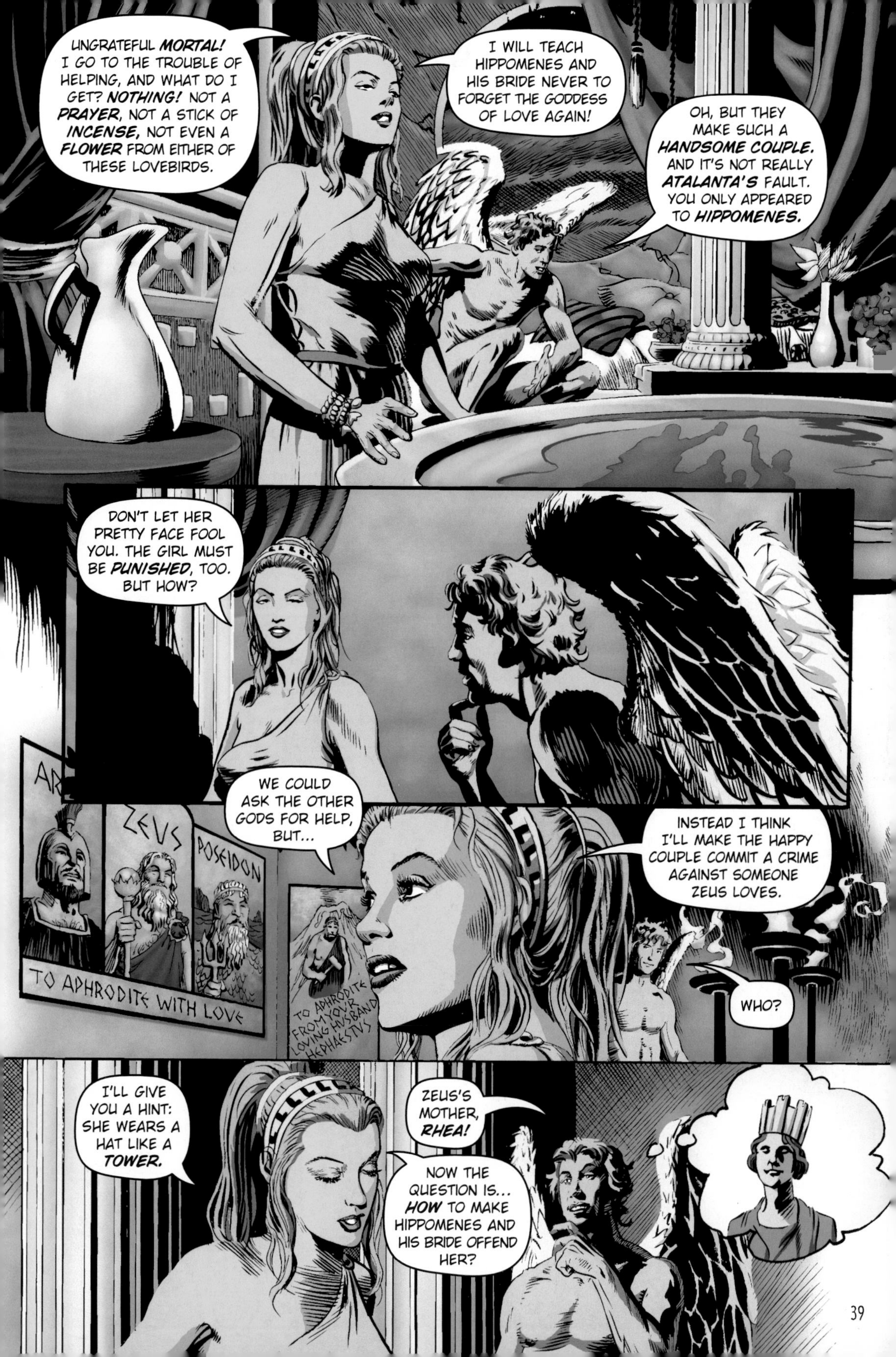
UNGRATEFUL MORTAL! I GO TO THE TROUBLE OF HELPING, AND WHAT DO I GET? NOTHING! NOT A PRAYER, NOT A STICK OF INCENSE, NOT EVEN A FLOWER FROM EITHER OF THESE LOVEBIRDS.
I WILL TEACH HIPPOMENES AND HIS BRIDE NEVER TO FORGET THE GODDESS OF LOVE AGAIN!
OH, BUT THEY MAKE SUCH A HANDSOME COUPLE. AND IT'S NOT REALLY ATALANTA'S FAULT. YOU ONLY APPEARED TO HIPPOMENES.
DON'T LET HER PRETTY FACE FOOL YOU. THE GIRL MUST BE PUNISHED, TOO. BUT HOW?
WE COULD ASK THE OTHER GODS FOR HELP, BUT...
ZEUS
POSEIDON
TO APHRODITE WITH LOVE
TO APHRODITE FROM YOUR LOVING HUSBAND HEPHAESTUS
INSTEAD I THINK I'LL MAKE THE HAPPY COUPLE COMMIT A CRIME AGAINST SOMEONE ZEUS LOVES.
WHO?
I'LL GIVE YOU A HINT: SHE WEARS A HAT LIKE A TOWER.
ZEUS'S MOTHER, RHEA!
NOW THE QUESTION IS... HOW TO MAKE HIPPOMENES AND HIS BRIDE OFFEND HER?

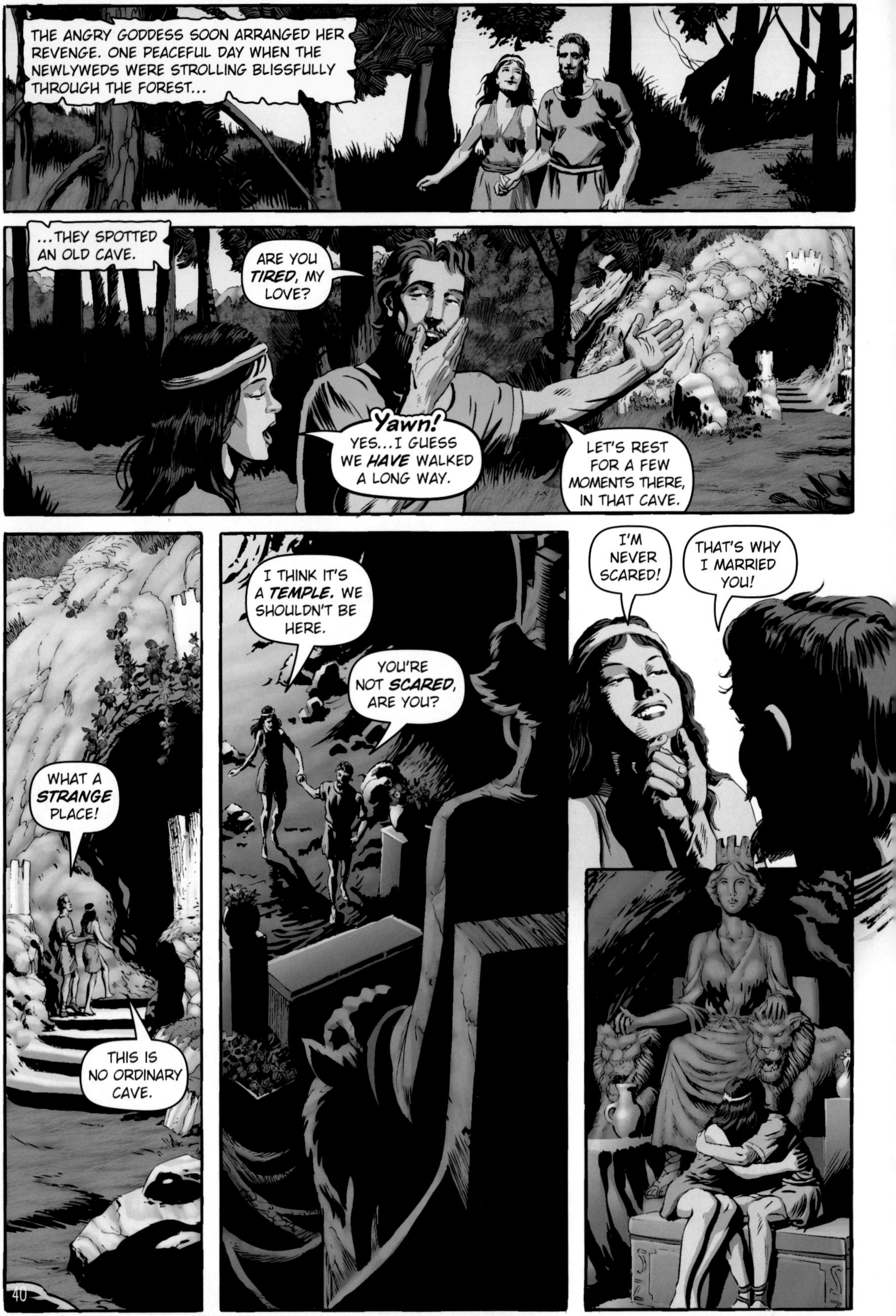
THE ANGRY GODDESS SOON ARRANGED HER REVENGE. ONE PEACEFUL DAY WHEN THE NEWLYWEDS WERE STROLLING BLISSFULLY THROUGH THE FOREST...
...THEY SPOTTED AN OLD CAVE.
ARE YOU TIRED, MY LOVE?
Yawn! YES...I GUESS WE HAVE WALKED A LONG WAY.
LET'S REST FOR A FEW MOMENTS THERE, IN THAT CAVE.
WHAT A STRANGE PLACE!
THIS IS NO ORDINARY CAVE.
I THINK IT'S A TEMPLE. WE SHOULDN'T BE HERE.
YOU'RE NOT SCARED, ARE YOU?
I'M NEVER SCARED!
THAT'S WHY I MARRIED YOU!

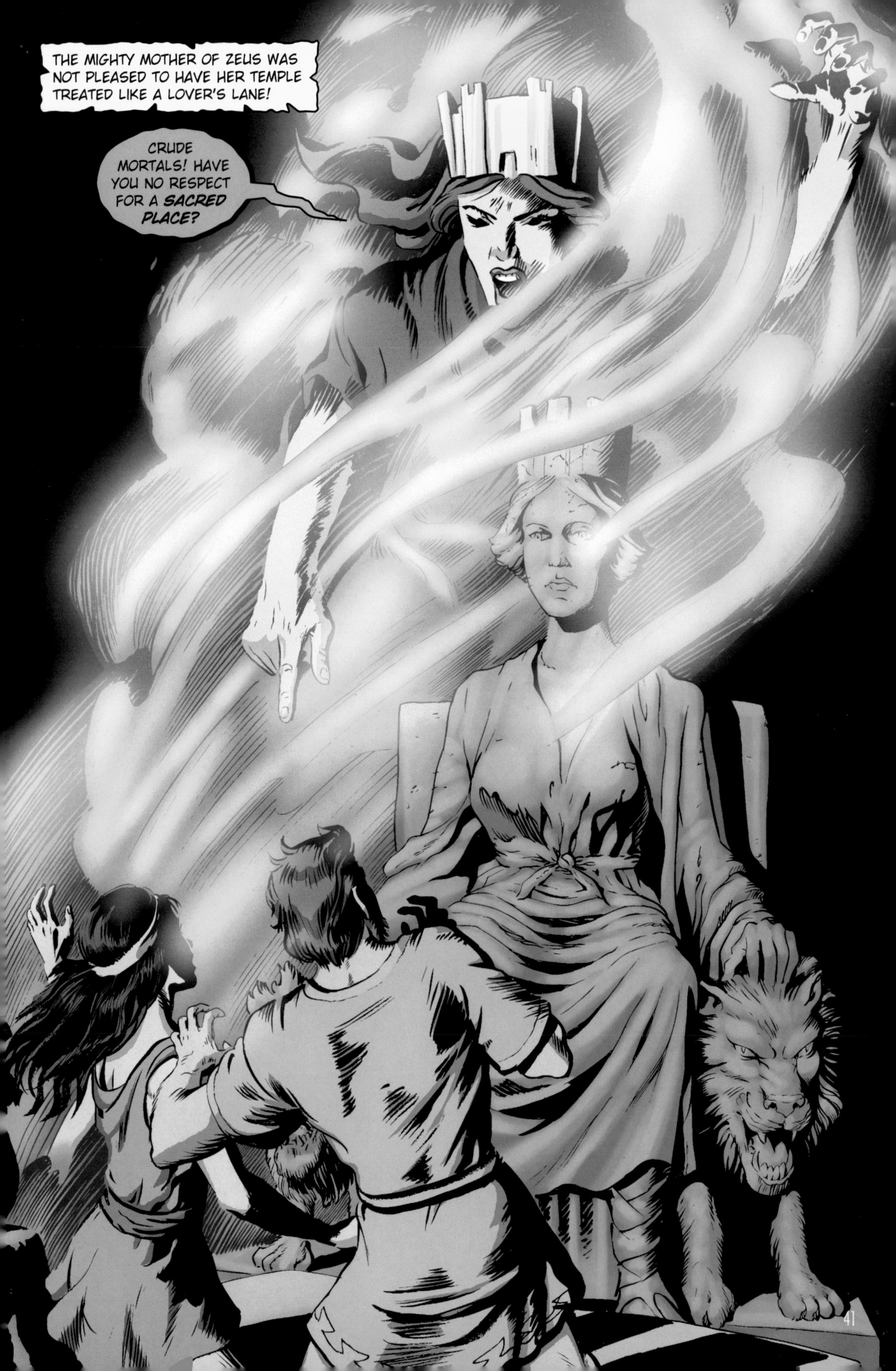
THE MIGHTY MOTHER OF ZEUS WAS NOT PLEASED TO HAVE HER TEMPLE TREATED LIKE A LOVER'S LANE!
CRUDE MORTALS! HAVE YOU NO RESPECT FOR A SACRED PLACE?

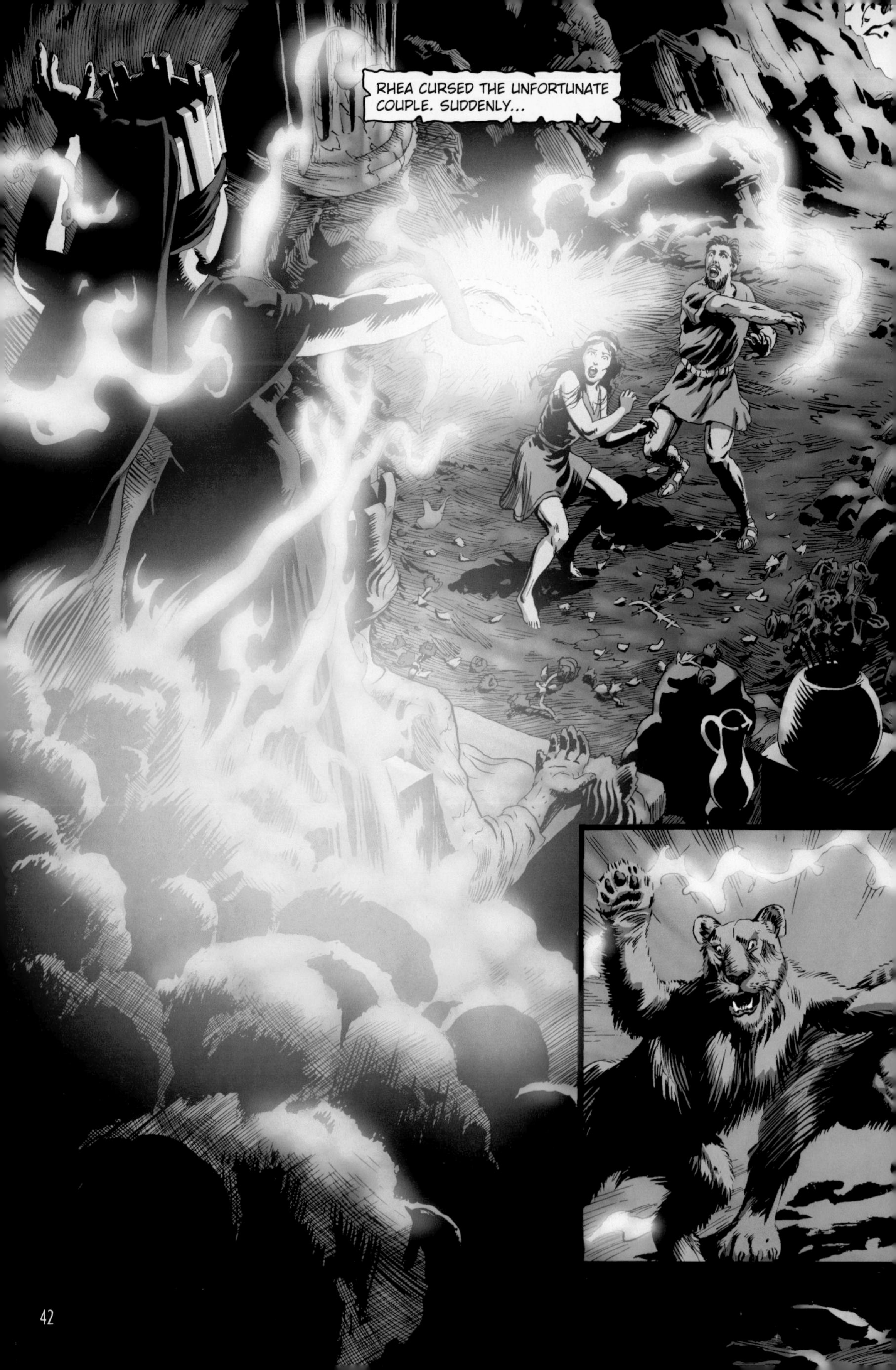
RHEA CURSED THE UNFORTUNATE COUPLE. SUDDENLY...

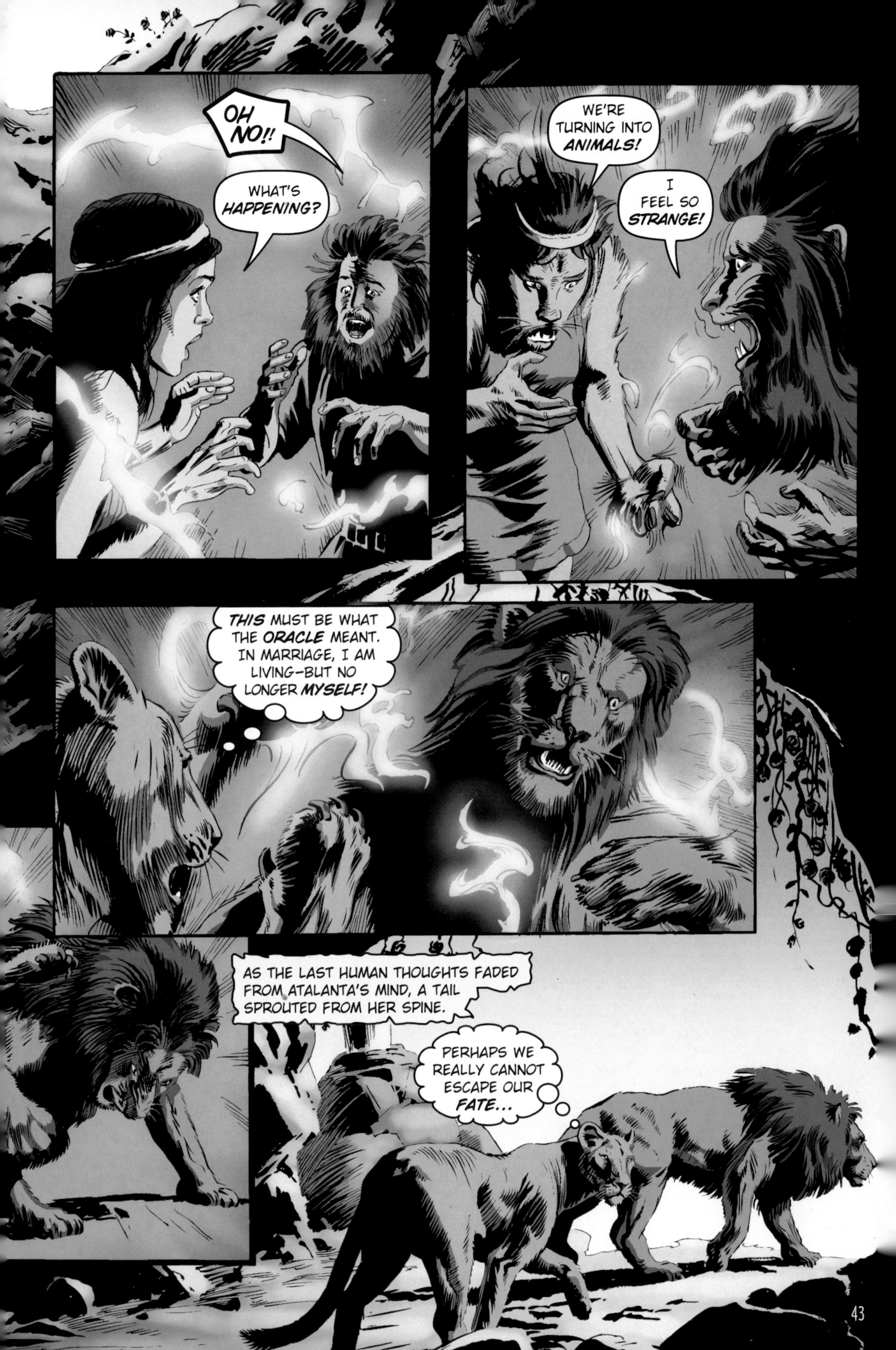
OH NO!!
WHAT'S HAPPENING?
WE'RE TURNING INTO ANIMALS!
I FEEL SO STRANGE!
THIS MUST BE WHAT THE ORACLE MEANT. IN MARRIAGE, I AM LIVING—BUT NO LONGER MYSELF!
AS THE LAST HUMAN THOUGHTS FADED FROM ATALANTA'S MIND, A TAIL SPROUTED FROM HER SPINE.
PERHAPS WE REALLY CANNOT ESCAPE OUR FATE...

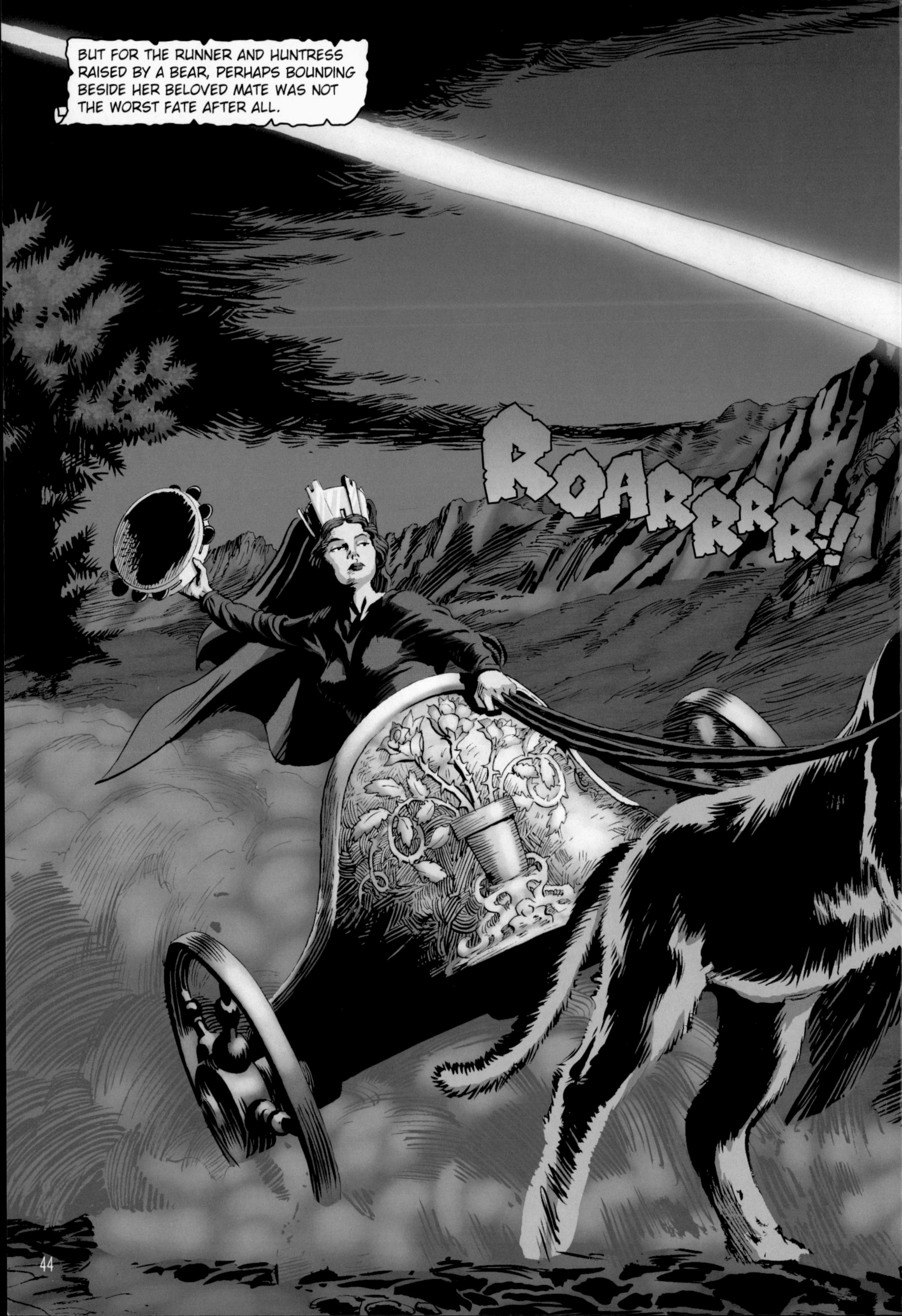
BUT FOR THE RUNNER AND HUNTRESS RAISED BY A BEAR, PERHAPS BOUNDING BESIDE HER BELOVED MATE WAS NOT THE WORST FATE AFTER ALL.
ROARRRR!!

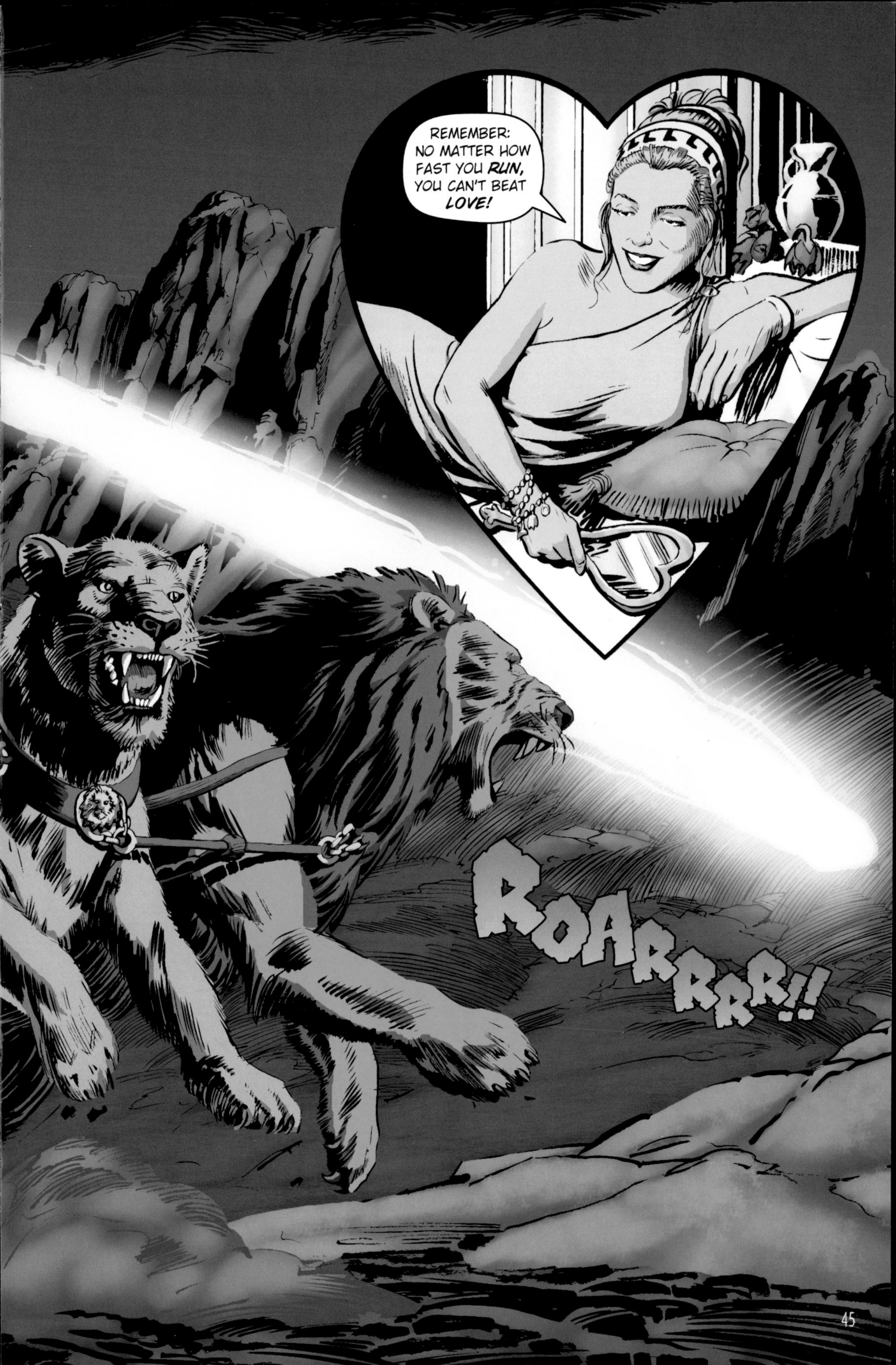
REMEMBER: NO MATTER HOW FAST YOU *RUN*, YOU CAN'T BEAT *LOVE!*
ROARRRRR!!

GLOSSARY AND PRONUNCIATION GUIDE

APHRODITE (a-fruh-*dye*-tee): the Greek goddess of love

APOLLO (uh-*pahl*-oh): the Greek god of music, poetry, prophecy, and light. Apollo is the twin brother of Artemis.

ARTEMIS (*ar*-tuh-mis): the Greek goddess of hunting and the wilderness, as well as of childbirth. She is Apollo's twin sister.

ATALANTA (at-uh-*lan*-tuh): the great huntress of ancient Greece. Atalanta was also a great athlete.

ATHENA (uh-*thee*-nuh): the Greek goddess of wisdom

CALYDON (*ka*-luh-dahn): a city in central Greece where Atalanta and many Greek heroes fought the Calydonian boar

DELPHI (*del*-fy): a city in central Greece where the oracle of the god Apollo is located

EROS (*air*-ahs): Aphrodite's son and the god of love

FATES: the three goddesses who oversee human fate. Clotho spins the thread that represents a person's life, Lachesis measures it, and Atropos cuts it with her scissors.

HERA (*hehr*-uh): the Greek goddess of marriage and childbirth who is married to Zeus

HIPPOMENES (hih-*pahm*-uh-neez): Atalanta's suitor. During the race for her hand, he tricks her with the golden apples and wins the race against her, after which they are married.

MELEAGER (meh-lee-*ay*-jur): the son of King Oeneus of Calydon

MOUNT OLYMPUS (oh-*lim*-pus): the home of the Greek gods and goddesses

ORACLE (*ohr*-uh-kul): in ancient Greece, a priestess or other person through whom the gods were believed to communicate

RHEA (*ree*-uh): the mother of Zeus and other major gods

ZEUS (zoos): the highest Greek god and the ruler of Mount Olympus

FURTHER READING, WEBSITES, AND MOVIES

Clash of the Titans. DVD. Directed by Desmond Davis. Burbank, CA: Warner Home Video, 1981. Rereleased 2004. Although this movie does not tell Atalanta's story, it does feature Aphrodite, Zeus, and other gods who affected her fate. It describes the hero Perseus and his quest to kill the Gorgon Medusa.

Day, Nancy. *Your Travel Guide to Ancient Greece*. Minneapolis: Twenty-First Century Books, 2001. Day prepares readers for a trip back to classical Greece, including which cities to visit, how to get around, what to wear, and how to fit in with the locals.

Encyclopedia of Greek Mythology: Atalanta.
http://www.mythweb.com/encyc/entries/atalanta.html
With engaging cartoons and easy-to-read text, this kid-friendly site explores the story of Atalanta and also of many other Greek heroes and heroines.

Macdonald, Fiona. *Gods and Goddesses in the Daily Life of the Ancient Greeks*. New York: Peter Bedrick Books, 2001. Macdonald provides an introduction to the traditions and religious beliefs of the ancient Greeks. Using photographs, illustrations, and detailed diagrams, the book looks at how these beliefs affected daily routines, entertainment and literature, and events such as birth and death.

Spinner, Stephanie. *Quiver*. New York: Knopf, 2002. This short novel is a retelling of the Atalanta myth for young readers.

CREATING *ATALANTA: THE RACE AGAINST DESTINY*

In creating the story, authors Justine and Ron Fontes drew upon many resources, including Edith Hamilton's classic ***Mythology*** and the widely respected ***Myths of the Greeks and Romans*** by professor and classics scholar Michael Grant. Artist Thomas Yeates used historical and traditional sources to shape the story's visual details—from images on ancient Greek vases to sculpture and other artwork. David Mulroy of the University of Wisconsin-Milwaukee ensured the accuracy of the story's historical and visual details. Together, the text and the art bring to life this story from ancient Greece.

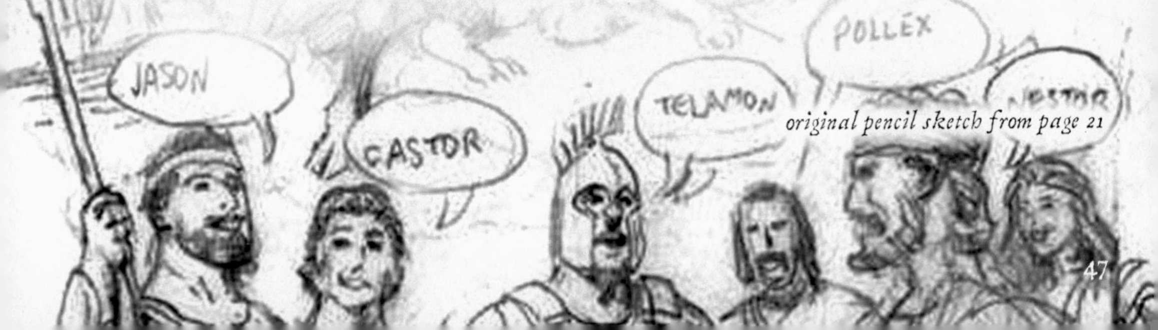
JASON
CASTOR
TELAMON
POLLEX
original pencil sketch from page 21

INDEX

ABOUT THE AUTHORS AND THE ARTIST

RON AND JUSTINE FONTES met at a publishing house in New York City. Ron worked for the comic book department, and Justine was an editorial assistant in children's books. Together they have written nearly 500 children's books, in every format from board books to historical novels. From their home in Maine, the Fonteses publish *critter news*, a strictly-for-fun newsletter. They also launched Sonic Comics with their first graphic novel *Tales of the Terminal Diner*, a unique anthology with continuing characters. Other published projects include *The Trojan Horse: The Fall of Troy*, *Demeter & Persephone: Spring Held Hostage*, and *The Wooden Sword*. Life-long library lovers, the Fonteses long to write 1,001 books before retiring to read.

THOMAS YEATES began his art training in high school and continued at Utah State University and Sacramento State. Subsequently, he was a member of the first class at Joe Kubert's School, a trade program for aspiring comic book artists in New Jersey. Yeates has worked as an illustrator for DC Comics, Marvel, Dark Horse, and many other companies, drawing Tarzan, Zorro, the Swamp Thing, Timespirits, Captain America, and Conan. For the Graphic Myths and Legends series, he illustrated *King Arthur: Excalibur Unsheathed* and *Robin Hood: Outlaw of Sherwood Forest*. Yeates lives in northern California with his wife and daughter.